VOYAGE AROUND MY ROOM

"Count Xavier de Maistre has come down to us as one of those men whose presence serves to console us for a great many disappointments in literature and gently reconciles us with human nature. . . . One derives both pleasure and benefit from more than a few of his naïve and subtle judgments."

Saint-Beuve

VOYAGE AROUND MY ROOM

Selected Works of Xavier de Maistre

Introduction by Richard Howard

•

Preface by Joseph de Maistre

•

Translated,
with notes and chronology,
by Stephen Sartarelli

A NEW DIRECTIONS BOOK

Manufactured in the United States of America
New Directions Books are printed on acid-free paper.
First published as a New Directions Paperbook 791 in 1994
Published simultaneously in Canada by Penguin Books Canada
Limited

Library of Congress Cataloging-in-Publication Data

Maistre, Xavier de, 1763–1852.
   [Selections. English. 1994]
   Voyage around my room : selected works of
   Xavier de Maistre /
introduction by Richard Howard ; preface by Joseph de Maistre ;
translated, with notes and chronology by Stephen Sartarelli.
   p.   cm.
   ISBN: 0–8112–1280–7
   1. Maistre, Xavier, 1763–1852—Translations into English.
I. Sartarelli, Stephen, 1954—   II. Title.
PQ2342.M3A27   1994
843′.6—dc20
                       94–17834
                       CIP

New Directions Books are published for James Laughlin
by New Directions Publishing Corporation,
80 Eighth Avenue, New York 10011

CONTENTS

INTRODUCTION

Invitation to the Voyages of Xavier de Maistre

A

In 1790, Count Xavier de Maistre, a twenty-seven-year-old Savoyard officer stationed in Turin, fought a duel with a Piedmontese officer and was put under house arrest for forty-two days, an interval during which he wrote a text to beguile the languors of his solitude—having hitherto shown no trace of a literary vocation—and in 1794 he left the manuscript of *Voyage autour de ma chambre* in Lausanne with his older brother Joseph, who published it there the following year without the author's knowledge. Two centuries later we are astonished by the many anomalies which these circumstances present to current notions of authorship, of intellectuality, and of what we might call the military necessity. Our amazement at the oddities of the young count's career will be enhanced by our discovery that he was an early enthusiast of the brothers Montgolfier, that he flew in a hot-air balloon at the age of twenty-one, and that he described the ascent in a ''Letter Containing an Account of the Aerostatic Experiment of Chambéry'' (1784).

B

In 1798 Count Xavier, delighted by his un-suspected status as a *littérateur,* began writing a se-quel, *Expédition nocturne autour de ma chambre,* which his brother advised against publishing—"according to the Spanish proverb, Part II is always bad''—and which remained in manuscript until 1825, four years after Joseph's death, when the (in-accurately titled) *Oeuvres complètes de Xavier de Maistre* appeared in Paris with considerable success. Subsequently these brief texts have been accorded a certain classical, or academic, success; they are *ré-cits,* a genre which has long been appreciated in France (from Constant to Camus, with brilliant illus-trations by Gide and Blanchot) and exemplified as well in Russia (*Notes from Underground,* for exam-ple), in Italy, and of course in England, where the personal essay invariably threatens to spill over into this protean form. A *récit* is a sort of dramatic mono-logue in prose concerned with the problematics of narrative, questioning the nature of such pronouns as ''I,'' ''he,'' and ''you,'' and given, as Northrop Frye has determined, to notions of literature as pro-cess rather than as product. De Maistre's versions are among the liveliest and the most lenient in the repertoire.

C

In 1810 Count Xavier—whose brother, now plenipotentiary envoy of the Kingdom of Sardinia to St. Petersburg, has arranged for him to be appointed director of the Admiralty Museum while serving as a colonel in the tsar's army—attends a gathering where, during a discussion of leprosy in Scripture, someone asserts that the disease no longer exists; Xavier excitedly describes a leper he had known in Aosta. Joseph encourages him to write the account, which is published the following year as *Le Lépreux de la Cité d'Aoste,* along with the *Voyage autor de ma chambre,* in St. Petersburg.

D

It is necessary to recall the qualities of this over-whelming older brother, whose genius for provocation was matched only by the eloquence of his umbrage and the dogmatic vehemence of his contempt. Embodying Catholic reaction against the doctrines of the *philosophes,* Joseph de Maistre, in a series of scathing works beginning with *Considérations sur la France* (1796) and culminating in *Du Pape* (1819) and *Les Soirées de Saint-Pétersbourg* (1820), brandished anathemas with enthusiastic cruelty, and raised his repudiations of science, of progress, of democracy, and of tolerance to the dignity of scandal. It is to him that the roots of French fascism descend, and it is no surprise to find this apologist for capital punishment praised by Baudelaire, who once said that "De Maistre and Edgar Poe taught me to reason." Nothing of his aggressive, indeed his insolent lucidity is shared by the younger brother, but the charm and amenity of Xavier's texts provide a kind of responsive alternative to the arrogance of Joseph's prejudices.

E

In 1838 Count Xavier—having served with distinction in the Russian armies against Napoleon ("the man from Hell"), whose retreat in 1812 his letters eloquently describe; having married a Russian woman in 1813 and had a son in 1817; having given up his military career in 1816 and having lived a tranquil family life in St. Petersburg for ten years; having returned to Italy in 1826, after his brother's death in 1821, leading in his beloved Turin the life of an important man of the world—visits Paris for the first time (and meets Sainte-Beuve, who consecrates his literary success by an essay in 1839).

Savoy, Sardinia, Switzerland, Italy, Russia: in pre-Bonaparte Europe it is possible to express (and to feel) allegiances to all these protonational entities and still be (or become) a French writer, readily acknowledged, even proclaimed, as Xavier de Maistre has been, a characteristic practitioner of a certain engaging resonance, informal and even capricious, yet immitigably a part of the realm of "polite letters."

F

Virtually unknown to English-speaking readers today (though there have been earlier translations), *Le Voyage autour de ma chambre* flaunts its filiations (as in Chapter XIX, Chapter XXVIII) with the powerful model of deviation and even of subversion established by Sterne, a resonance that would be echoed throughout Europe and even in Latin America (from Goncharov to Machado de Assis); Sainte-Beuve detected even more of the *grace souriante et sensible* of Charles Lamb in these whimsical chapters, and managed, as well, to find in De Maistre's incidental verses something of the *lucky* innocence of La Fontaine, as in these first lines of his *épitaphe;*

> Under this gray stone, Xavier lies
> To whom everything was a surprise:
> Where did the wind come from, he wondered,
> And why was it that Jupiter thundered?

How flabbergasting it is that the young count should also have been a passionate admirer of Ossian!

Certainly the point of Xavier's *voyages* is not to keep us wondering what will happen next, but what the author will think of next: this is a literature of the irregular and unpredictable, tending to brief or even fragmentary utterance. The qualities of consciousness are recessive, and operate in flashes, in explosions of insight which are not likely to sustain any sort of continuous development.

But such explosions are often of an astonishing

brilliance in themselves, unlikely to quit the memory, and they foreshadow, so to speak, much that has been more laboriously and systematically discovered by our ulterior science, our psychology of the unconscious. I refer, for example, to what in Chapter VI De Maistre calls his "system of *the soul and the beast.*" Here he accounts, in the blithest fashion, for that entire Faustian division of the self which was to become one of the great tragic themes in Western culture:

> I have conducted I know not how many experiments on the union of these two heterogeneous creatures. For example, I have clearly determined that the soul can command obedience from the beast, and that, by an unfortunate reciprocity, the latter can very often compel the soul to act against her will. . . . When you are reading a book, Monsieur, and a thought more agreeable than the rest suddenly enters your mind, your soul clings to it at once and forgets the book. As your eyes mechanically follow the words and lines, you reach the end of the page without understanding or remembering what you have just read; and this is because your soul, having ordered her companion to do the reading in her place, did not inform him that she was about to absent herself briefly, and thus the *other* continued reading while your soul no longer listened.

With what imperturbable amenity De Maistre plays on this theme, that we are not always ourselves!

How wickedly he articulates some of the consequences of such dichotomy, such role-playing:

> Gentlemen: Never forget that on the day of a ball, your mistress is no longer yours.
>
> The moment the dressing begins, the lover becomes nothing more than a husband: the ball alone is the lover. . . . have no illusions: if she shows great delight in seeing you at the ball, it is not as a lover that you give such pleasure, for you are a husband: it is because you are part of the ball, and because you are, therefore, a fraction of her new conquest, a *decimal* of a lover . . .

But the perceptions are never permitted to extend themselves into anything so formal as a method, a system. Even the direst insights are playfully made, glancing, hit or miss. And the game of intimate relations—identity's Marivaudage—is played to the bittersweet end, relentless, heartbreaking. It is an extraordinary moment of equilibrium, somewhere between the Misanthrope and Manfred, that Xavier de Maistre occupies, a moment which merits our modern perscrutation.

G

Having returned to Russia in 1839, two years after the much-lamented death of his twenty-year-old son, Count Xavier established a salon which became the meeting-place of French society in the capital, until his wife died in 1851, leaving him despondent. In 1852 Xavier de Maistre died in St. Petersburg at the age of eighty-nine, having survived his entire family, his century, and in some sense himself.

RICHARD HOWARD

VOYAGE AROUND MY ROOM
(1794)

Dans maint auteur, de science profonde,
J'ai lu qu'on perd à trop courir le monde.

Louis Gresset*

CHAPTER I

How glorious it is to blaze a new trail, and suddenly to appear in learned society, a book of discoveries in one's hand, like an unforeseen comet flashing through space!

—No, I will no longer keep my book *in petto:** here it is, gentlemen. Read it. I have just completed a forty-two-day voyage around my room. The fascinating observations I made and the endless pleasures I experienced along the way made me wish to share my travels with the public; and the certainty of having something useful to offer convinced me to do so. Words cannot describe the satisfaction I feel in my heart when I think of the infinite number of unhappy souls for whom I am providing a sure antidote to boredom and a palliative to their ills. For the pleasure of traveling around one's room is beyond the reach of man's restless jealousy: it depends not on one's material circumstance.

Indeed, is there anyone so wretched, so forlorn as not to have some sort of garret in which to withdraw

*Asterisks refer to explanatory notes starting at page 195.

and hide from the world? For such is all that is required for travel.

I am certain that all sensible men will adopt my system, regardless of disposition or temperament. Whether they be miserly or prodigal, rich or poor, young or old, born in the torrid zone or near the pole, they can travel as I do. Indeed, in the vast family of men teeming on the surface of the earth, there is not one, no, not a single one (among those living in rooms, that is) who, upon reading this book, could possibly refuse to approve the new manner of travel that I am introducing to the world.

Chapter II

I could begin the praise of my voyage by saying that it cost me nothing. This point merits some attention. It will, at first, be extolled and celebrated by people of middling circumstances; yet there is another class of people with whom it is even more certain to enjoy great success, for the same reason, that it costs nothing. And who would these people be? Need you even ask? Why, the rich, of course. And in what respect would this new manner of travel not also be suitable for the infirm? They need not fear the inclemency of the elements or the seasons. As for the faint of heart, they will be safe from bandits, and need not fear encountering any precipices or holes in the road. Thousands of people who, before me, had never dared to travel, and others who had been unable, and still others who had never dreamed of it, will now, after my example, undertake to do so. Would even the most indolent of creatures hesitate to set out with me in search of pleasures that will cost him neither effort nor money? Buck up, then; we're on our way. Follow me, all you whom humiliation in love or neglect in friendship confines to your apartments, far from the pettiness and treachery of your fellow men. Let all the wretched, the sick, and the bored follow me—let all the lazy people of the world rise *en masse;*—and you, whose brain is aboil with sinister plans of reform; you, who in your boudoir are contemplating renouncing the world *in order to live;* gentle anchorites of an evening, you too, come, heed my call and forget those dark ideas; you are losing time for pleasure, while gaining none for wisdom; be so good as to accompany me on my voyage, we shall travel by short stages, laughing all along the way at travelers who have seen Rome and Paris.—Nothing can stop us; and abandoning ourselves gaily to our fancy, we shall follow it wherever it wishes to take us.

CHAPTER III

There are so many curious people in this world.—
I am convinced that some would like to know why
my voyage around my room lasted forty-two days
instead of forty-three or some other length of time.
But how can I impart this to the reader, if I myself do
not know? All I can say with any assurance is that if
this work is too long for his liking, it was not within
my power to shorten it: a traveler's vanity not with-
standing, I would have been content with a single
chapter. I was, it is true, quite pleased and amused to
stay in my room; but I was not, alas, free to come out
at will. Indeed, I believe that without the intervention of certain powerful persons interested in my
case, and for whom my gratitude is most keen, I
should have had all the time I needed to bring out an
in-folio volume, so disposed in my favor were the
protectors who sent me on my voyage around my
room.

And yet, sensible reader, note how wrong these
men were, and try, if you can, to grasp the logic that
I am about to set forth to you.

What could be more natural and proper than to
engage in mutual slaughter with someone who has
inadvertently stepped on your foot or blurted out a
few stinging remarks in a moment of spite occasioned by your own indiscretion, or who has had the
misfortune of catching your mistress's fancy?

You go into a meadow, and there, as Nicole did

with the Bourgeois Gentilhomme, you try to thrust in quarte while he parries in tierce; and, so that vengeance will be guaranteed and total, you expose your chest to him unprotected, and run the risk of being killed by your enemy to avenge yourself on him.— Nothing could be more logical, and yet there are people who disapprove of this laudable custom! Yet equally logical as the rest is that these same disapproving people, who want us to consider it a grave misdeed, would reserve still harsher treatment for anyone who refused to commit it. To conform to their opinion, more than one unhappy wretch has lost his reputation and livelihood; consequently, when one has the misfortune to become involved in what is called an *affair of honor,* it may not be ill-advised to draw lots to determine whether one should carry it out according to law or according to custom; and since the law and the custom are in contradiction, the judges themselves could decide upon their sentence with a toss of the dice. One must, no doubt, look to a decision of this sort to explain why and how my voyage lasted exactly forty-two days.

CHAPTER IV

My room is situated at forty-five degrees latitude, according to the measurements of Father *Beccaria*.* It runs from east to west, and forms a rectangle that is thirty-six paces around, keeping well nigh to the walls. My voyage, however, will encompass a great deal more; for I shall often walk across it lengthwise and breadthwise, and diagonally too, following no rule or method.—I shall even zigzag this way and that, and follow every line possible in geometry, if necessary. I do not care much for people who so control their steps and ideas, who say, *"Today I will pay three visits, write four letters, and finish the piece I have begun."*—My soul is so open to every manner of idea, taste, and sentiment, it avidly takes in everything that turns up! . . . —And why should it refuse any of the delights scattered along the difficult path of life? They are so rare, so few and far between, that one would have to be mad not to stop, indeed to stray from one's path, to gather every one that is within reach. And there is none more enticing, in my opinion, than to follow the trail of one's ideas, as the hunter stalks his quarry, without keeping to any one course. I too, when traveling in my room, rarely follow a straight line! I go from my table toward a painting hung in a corner, and from there I set off obliquely for the door; yet although in setting out my intention is to reach that spot, if I happen to encounter my armchair along the way,

8

without hesitation I settle right down into it.—What a splendid piece of furniture an armchair is, of utmost importance and usefulness for every contemplative man. During those long winter evenings, it is often sweet and always advisable to stretch out luxuriously in one, far from the din of the crowds. A good fire, a few books, some quills—what excellent antidotes to boredom! And what a pleasure then to forget your books and quills and to poke the fire, relinquishing your thoughts to some pleasant meditation—or composing some rhymes to amuse your friends: the hours slide over you and fall silently into eternity, and you do not even feel their melancholy passing.

CHAPTER V

Heading north from my armchair, we discover my bed, which sits at the back of the room and creates a most agreeable perspective: it is most felicitously situated, receiving the morning sun's first rays as they shine through my curtains.—On lovely summer days, I see them advance along the white wall as the sun slowly rises; the elm trees outside my window break them up in a thousand different ways, sending them rippling across my pink and white bed, which everywhere casts a charming glow from their reflection.—I hear the confused twitter of the swallows that have made a home of the building's roof, and the other birds that inhabit the elms: a thousand happy ideas fill my mind, and no man alive enjoys an awakening so pleasant and peaceful as mine.

I must admit that I love to savor those sweet moments, and I always prolong as much as possible the pleasure of meditating in the sweet warmth of my bed.—Is there any theater that better quickens the imagination, that more effectively awakens thoughts of tenderness, than the piece of furniture in which I sometimes find oblivion?—Modest reader, have no fear;—but shall I never be able to speak of the happiness of a lover who, for the first time, takes a virtuous wife into his arms? What ineffable pleasure, which my unhappy fate condemns me never to taste! Is it not in a bed that a mother, drunk with the joy of her child's birth, forgets her pain? It is here that the imaginary pleasures, the fruits of fancy and hope, come to stir us.—And it is in this cradle of delight that we forget, for one half of our life's duration, the sorrows of the other half.—Yet what a host of thoughts both pleasant and sad rush all at once into my brain! What a bewildering mix of frightful and delightful situations!—A bed witnesses our birth and it witnesses our death: it is the ever-changing theater where the human species enacts, by turns, engaging dramas, ridiculous farces, and horrible tragedies.— It is a cradle decked with flowers;—it is love's throne;—it is a sepulcher.

CHAPTER VI

This chapter is strictly for metaphysicians. It will shed the greatest possible light on the nature of man; it is a prism through which we shall soon be able to analyze and break down man's faculties, separating his animal powers from the pure light of intelligence.

It would be impossible for me to explain how and why I burned my fingers when taking the first steps of my voyage, without first explaining to the reader, in the greatest of detail, my system of *the soul and the beast*.—This metaphysical discovery, moreover, has such great bearing on my thoughts and actions that it would be most difficult to understand this book if I did not provide the key to it at the very beginning.

I have noticed, through many and sundry observations, that man is made up of a soul and a beast.—These two beings are absolutely distinct, yet so contained within one another, or rather on top of one another, that the soul must in some way be superior to the beast to be able to make such a distinction.

An old professor once told me (that's as much as I can remember) that Plato called matter the *other*. That's quite good, yet I would rather give that quintessential name to the beast that is united with our soul. For that substance is the real *other* and pesters us in a most distressing manner. It is rather frequently observed that man is twofold, but this is, they say, because he is made up of a soul and a body; and this body is accused of I know not how many dreadful things, quite inappropriately I am sure, since it is as incapable of feeling as it is of thinking. The real culprit is the beast, that sentient being utterly distinct from the soul, that veritable *individual* that has his own separate existence, tastes, inclinations and will, and is superior to the other animals only because he happens to be a little more well-bred and endowed with more perfect organs.

Ladies and Gentlemen, be as proud of your intelligence as you please, but beware of that *other*—especially when you are together.

I have conducted I know not how many experiments on the union of these two heterogeneous creatures. For example, I have clearly determined that the soul can command obedience from the beast, and that, by an unfortunate reciprocity, the latter can very often compel the soul to act against her will. According to the rules, the one has legislative power, the other executive power; but very often these powers oppose each other.—The great skill of a man of genius lies in knowing how to bring his beast up well, so that he may go his own way in the world while the soul, released from this distressing intimacy, raises herself to the heavens.*

But let me clarify this with an example.

When you are reading a book, Monsieur, and a thought more agreeable than the rest suddenly enters your mind, your soul clings to it at once and forgets the book. As your eyes mechanically follow the words and lines, you reach the end of the page without understanding or remembering what you have just read; and this is because your soul, having ordered her companion to do the reading in her place, did not inform him that she was about to absent herself briefly, and thus the *other* continued reading while your soul no longer listened.

CHAPTER VII

Does that not seem clear to you? Here is another example.

One day last summer I was on my way to the Court. I had been painting all morning, and my soul, taking pleasure in meditating on painting, left it to the beast to transport me to the royal palace.

"What a sublime art painting is!" my soul was thinking. "Happy is the man moved by the spectacle of nature who is not obliged to make paintings for a living; who does not paint solely as a pastime, but rather, when struck by the majesty of a beautiful countenance or the wonderful play of the light as it blends into a thousand shades on a human face, strives in his works to approximate nature's sublime effects! And happier still the painter who, summoned to his solitary promenades by his love for the landscape, can express on canvas the sadness inspired in him by a shaded thicket or an empty plain.

His creations imitate and reproduce nature; he invents new seas and dark caverns the sun has never known: at his command, shady groves, always green, arise from nothing; heaven's blue is mirrored in his paintings. With his art he can roil the winds and make tempests roar. At other times he presents to the spectator's astonished eye the splendid landscapes of ancient Sicily: one sees frightened nymphs fleeing through the reeds, pursued by a satyr; temples of majestic architecture rise proudly above the sacred forest surrounding them: the imagination loses its way along the silent paths of this ideal land; the bluish distance blends into the sky, and the whole landscape, mirrored in the waters of a tranquil river, creates a spectacle that no language can describe.''—As my soul was reflecting thus, the *other* continued on his way, and God knows where he was going!—Instead of repairing to the court, as he had been ordered to do, he drifted so far to port that by the time my soul caught up, he was at Mme de *Hautcastel*'s front door, a half-mile from the king's palace.

I shall leave it to the reader to imagine what would have happened had I let my beast enter, alone, the house of so lovely a lady.

Chapter VIII

If it is useful and agreeable to have a soul so disengaged from matter that one can let her travel alone as one sees fit, this faculty also has its inconveniences. It was, for example, to blame for the burn I mentioned a few chapters back.—Customarily I leave to my beast the task of preparing my breakfast: he toasts and slices my bread, makes excellent coffee, and often drinks it without the participation of my soul, unless the latter wishes to amuse herself while watching the *other* work, but that happens rarely, and is very difficult to carry out; for it is easy, when one is performing a mechanical operation, to have one's mind on something else entirely, but it is extremely difficult to watch oneself working, so to speak, or—to put it more clearly in terms of my system—to use one's soul to observe the working of the beast without taking part.—For that is the most stunning metaphysical *tour de force* that man can perform.

I had laid my tongs down on the embers, to toast the bread, and a little while later, as my soul was traveling, a flaming log suddenly rolled onto the hearth—my poor beast set his hand to the tongs, and I burned my fingers.

Chapter IX

I hope that in the preceding chapters I have set forth my ideas well enough to give the reader food for thought and enable him to make discoveries of his own in this luminous realm. He could not help but be pleased with himself should he succeed one day in making his soul travel all by herself; the delights that this ability will bring to him will more than outweigh the misunderstandings that might result from it. Indeed, could there be any joy more gratifying than that of thus stretching one's existence, of inhabiting the earth and the heavens at once, of doubling, as it were, one's being?—Is it not man's eternal and forever unfulfilled wish to increase his power and abilities, to be where he is not, to recall the past and to live in the future? He wants to command armies and preside over academies; he wants to be worshiped by beautiful women; yet if he has all this, he misses the calm of the countryside, and envies the shepherd his cabin. His plans and hopes are forever doomed to founder against the real sorrows inherent in human nature: he cannot find happiness.—A quarter of an hour's travel with me will show him the way.

Ah, but why does he not leave these miserable cares, the torment of ambition, to the *other*?—Come, unhappy wretch! Try to break out of your prison and, from the sky where I will take you, amidst the heavenly orbs and the empyrean, look down upon your beast cast into the world, as he beats the path of fortune and honor all alone; see how solemnly he walks among men: the rabble steps aside in respect. And take my word, none shall ever notice that he is alone; that is the least concern of the mob in whose midst he moves; little do they care whether or not he has a soul, whether or not he thinks.—Hundreds of passionate women will love him madly unawares; and he can even, without the aid of your soul, raise himself to the highest station, the pinnacle of success.—In short, I should not be at all surprised if, upon our return from the empyrean, your soul, in going back home, found herself inside the beast of a great lord.

CHAPTER X

Let no one think that while describing my voyage around my room, instead of keeping my word I have been roaming the countryside to make things easy on myself. That would be quite mistaken, for my voyage, indeed, continues apace, and while my soul, withdrawing within herself in the previous chapter, was traveling the tortuous meanders of metaphysics, I was actually in my armchair, having leaned backward to the point where the two front legs were raised a couple of inches from the floor; then, rocking sideways from left to right, and gaining ground, I had, little by little, nearly reached the wall—such is my mode of travel when not in a hurry—: there, my hand had instinctively seized the portrait of Mme de *Hautcastel,* and the *other* then amused himself removing the dust that covered it.—He derived a quiet pleasure from this, a pleasure that made itself felt in my soul, even though she was lost in the vast reaches of the heavens. It is worthwhile to note that when the spirit is thus traveling through space, it remains bound to the senses by I know not what secret link; as a result, without interrupting its business, it can take part in the peaceful enjoyments of the *other;* yet if this pleasure grows beyond a certain point, or if the beast is struck by some unexpected sight, then the soul resumes her place with the swiftness of a lightning bolt.

This is what happened to me as I was cleaning the portrait.

As the cloth removed the dust and began to uncover the blond curls and the garland of roses crowning them, my soul, from the distant sun to which she had flown, felt a gentle quiver of delight and sympathetically shared my heart's joy. This joy became keener and less confused when the cloth, in a single stroke, revealed the stunning brow of that lovely countenance, and my soul made ready to quit the heavens to enjoy the spectacle. Even had she been in the Elysian Fields, or listening to a concert of cherubim, she would not have tarried half a second when her companion, taking ever greater interest in his work, thought to seize a wet sponge that had been

18

brought and to run this at once over the eyebrows and eyes,—over the nose,—the cheeks,—and that mouth.—Oh, God! my heart is racing:—over the chin, the bosom; it took but a moment, and the entire figure seemed to return to life, to emerge from oblivion.—My soul dashed headlong from the sky like a falling star; she found the *other* in a state of rapt ecstasy, and succeeded in augmenting this by taking part in it. This unusual, unforeseen situation made time and space disappear for me.—For an instant, I existed in the past; I grew younger, contrary to the laws of nature.—Yes, there she is: the beloved woman. It is she, none other: I see her smiling; she is about to speak, to tell me she loves me.—What a gaze! Come closer and let me clutch you to my breast, light of my life, my second existence! Come and share my transport and my happiness.—This moment was brief, but entrancing. Soon cold reason resumed its rule, and in the twinkling of an eye I aged an entire year: my heart grew cold, icy, and I found myself again among the indifferent crowd weighing down the planet.

CHAPTER XI

I must not get ahead of myself: in my eagerness to communicate to the reader my system of the soul and the beast, I left off the description of my bed sooner

19

than I ought to have done; once I have taken care of that, I shall resume my voyage at the very place where I interrupted it in the preceding chapter.—I ask you only to remember that we left *half of me* holding the portrait of Mme de *Hautcastel* very close to the wall, a few steps from my desk; I had forgotten, when talking about my bed, to advise every man who can to have a pink and white bed; there is no question but that colors have an influence on our moods, and may cheer us up or sadden us depending on their shades.—Pink and white are two colors given to pleasure and happiness.—In assigning them to the rose, nature gave it the crown of the realm of Flora.—And when the heavens wish to announce to the world the coming of a beautiful day, they color the clouds with that lovely hue at sunrise.

One day we were walking with difficulty up a steep path. The lovely Rosalie went ahead; her agility gave her wings, and we could not keep up with her. Suddenly, having reached the top of a little hill, she turned toward us to catch her breath and smiled at our slowness.—Never before, perhaps, had the two colors whose praise I sing been so triumphant. —Her burning cheeks, her coral lips, her gleaming teeth, her neck of alabaster against a verdant background, caught the attention of all. We had to stop to behold her: I will say nothing of her blue eyes, or of the glance she cast at us, for this would divert from my subject, and because I try to think of these things as little as possible. Let it suffice that I have provided the best possible example of the superiority of these two colors over all the rest, and of their effect on man's happiness.

I will go no further today. For what subject could I now discuss that would not seem utterly insipid? What idea is not effaced by that idea?—I do not even know when I shall be able to resume this work.—If I am to continue it, and if the reader wishes to see it completed, let him appeal to the angel who distributes thoughts and request that he cease mixing in the image of this little hill with the host of other disconnected thoughts that he throws my way at every moment.

Without this precaution, there is little hope for my voyage.

CHAPTER XII

.   .   .   .
.   .   .   .
.   .   .   .
.   .   .   .   .   . the little hill .   .   .   .   .
.   .   .   .
.   .   .   .
.   .   .   .

CHAPTER XIII

My efforts are in vain. We shall have to postpone matters, and sojourn here, willy-nilly. Think of it as a military stop.

CHAPTER XIV

I have said that I am particularly fond of meditating in the sweet warmth of my bed, and that its delightful color plays a large part in the pleasure I take in it.

To allow me this pleasure my valet has orders to enter my room one half-hour before I customarily get up. I hear him tread with a light step and *rummage* discreetly about my room, and this noise accords me the pleasure of feeling myself doze—a most exquisite enjoyment unknown to many! One is awake enough to perceive that one is not entirely so and to reckon vaguely that the time for business and worry is still in the day's hourglass. Ever so gradually my manservant becomes noisier: it is so hard for him to restrain himself! Nevertheless, the fateful hour draws near.—He looks at my watch and jingles the charms on its chain to let me know, but I turn a deaf ear to him; and there is no manner of quibble that I won't make with the poor man to prolong this wondrous moment.—I have a hundred preliminary orders to give him just to gain time. He is well aware that these orders, which I give to him rather peevishly, are merely pretexts for remaining in bed without making this desire apparent. He pretends not to notice, and I am most grateful to him for this.

When, at last, I have exhausted all my expedients, he advances to the center of the room and plants himself there, arms crossed, without moving.

It must be admitted that one could not protest my laziness with more wit or discretion. And indeed, I can never resist this tacit invitation: I stretch out my arms to show him that I have understood, and I sit up at once.

If the reader reflects a moment on my valet's conduct, he will realize that, in certain delicate matters such as the one at hand, simplicity and common sense are of infinitely greater value than the cleverest mind. I assure you that the most elaborate speech on the disadvantages of laziness would never convince me to get out of my bed so promptly as does the mute disapproval of Monsieur *Joanetti*.

A thoroughly decent fellow is Monsieur *Joanetti,* and of all men the most suitable for a traveler such as myself. He is accustomed to my soul's frequent voyages, and never laughs at the indiscretions of the *other;* in fact, he even gives him guidance sometimes when the *other* is alone, so that one could actually say that my beast is governed by two souls. When he dresses, for example, he lets him know, by a simple sign, that he is about to put on his stockings

inside out, or to don his coat before his jacket.—
More than once my soul has witnessed the amusing
sight of poor *Joannetti* running after the silly beast
under the porticoes of the citadel to tell him that he
has forgotten his hat, or, on another occasion, his
handkerchief.

One day (shall I admit it?), before the intervention
of this faithful servant, the scatterbrain was headed
to the Court without his sword, as fearlessly as a
master of ceremonies wielding his august wand.

CHAPTER XV

"Here, *Joanetti*," I said, "hang this portrait back
up."—He had helped me to clean it, and had no
more inkling of all the things that produced the chapter of the portrait than he did of what takes place on
the moon. It was he who, by his own initiative, had
brought me the wet sponge and who, with this apparently unexceptional gesture, had sent my soul ca-
reering a hundred million leagues in an instant. Instead of putting the picture back in its place, he held
it a moment, and examined it for himself.—Some
difficulty, or problem in need of resolution, gave
him an air of curiosity that I couldn't help but notice.

"Pray, tell," said I, "what is it about that portrait
that disturbs you?"

"Oh! nothing, Monsieur."

"Come now."

He stood it upright on one of the shelves on my writing-desk; then, backing up a few steps, he said, "I wish Monsieur would explain to me why this portrait always watches the observer, no matter what part of the room one may be in. In the morning, while I am making the bed, the face turns to me; and if I go to the window, she keeps looking at me, following me with her eyes all the way."

"And so, *Joanetti,*" said I, "if my room were full of people, that lovely lady would make eyes at everyone, and in all directions, at once?"

"I daresay she would, Monsieur."

"She would smile at the comers and goers even as she smiled at me?"

Joanetti gave no reply.—I stretched out in my armchair and, hanging my head, abandoned myself to meditations of the most serious sort.—What an illumination! Poor lover! While you languish far from your mistress, in whose heart you have perhaps already been replaced—while you gaze avidly upon her portrait and imagine yourself (at least in painting) to be alone in receiving a return glance, that perfidious effigy, as unfaithful as the original, casts her eyes upon all that surrounds her, and smiles at everyone.

This moral resemblance between certain portraits and their models is something that no philosopher, painter, or observer had ever noticed before. I am making discovery upon discovery.

CHAPTER XVI

Joanetti was still in the same position, awaiting the explanation he had asked of me. I raised my head from the folds of my *traveling coat* into which I had plunged it to meditate with greater ease, and after a moment of silence, to recover from the melancholy thoughts I had just had, "Don't you see, *Joanetti,*" I said, turning my armchair to face him, "don't you see that since a painting is a plane surface, the rays of light glancing from every point of this surface . . ."

Joanetti, hearing this explanation, opened his eyes so wide that the whites became entirely visible; moreover, his mouth was half open, and according to the famous Le Brun, these two movements in the human visage herald the last stages of astonishment. It was, no doubt, my beast who had embarked on that disquisition, for my soul was well aware that *Joanetti* had no idea what a plane surface was, much less a ray of light; and as the prodigious dilation of his eyelids had prompted me to withdraw within myself, I lowered my head anew into the collar of my traveling coat, burying it so deep therein that I nearly succeeded in hiding it entirely.

I decided to take my lunch in that very spot. The morning was wearing on; another step farther in my room would have carried my midday meal over into the night. I slid to the edge of my armchair, and setting both feet on the mantelpiece, I patiently awaited my meal.—What an exquisite position, that: it would, I think, be very difficult to find one that combines as many advantages and is as convenient for the inevitable stops one must make on a long voyage.

Rosine, my faithful dog, never fails at such moments to come and tug on the tails of my traveling coat, so that I will take her into my lap. There she finds a very comfortable bed all ready for her at the vertex of the angle formed by the two parts of my body: the letter V excellently represents my position. And if she finds I have not picked her up promptly enough, *Rosine* will leap up at me by herself. Often I find her there without even knowing how she got there; my hands then arrange themselves, of their own accord, in the manner that best suits her convenience, either from a natural sympathy between this beast and my own or by chance—but I do not believe in chance, that grim system: the word has no meaning. I would sooner believe in magnetism; I would sooner believe in Martinism*—no, *that,* I could never believe in.

So real are the relations that exist between these two animals, that when, with an utter absence of mind, I put my feet up on the mantelpiece, when the midday meal is still far off and I haven't a thought for *stopping to rest,* still *Rosine,* ever attentive to this movement of mine, betrays the pleasure she feels by lightly wagging her tail. Discretion keeps her in her place, and the *other,* noticing this, is grateful to her for it. And though he could never claim to know the causes thereof, a silent dialogue is established between the two, a pleasurable exchange of sensations, which could never be attributed to chance.

CHAPTER XVII

Let nobody criticize me for going into excessive detail; such is the manner of all travelers. When one sets off to climb Mont Blanc or goes to visit the great mouth of the tomb of *Empedocles,** one never fails to describe with utmost precision the most trifling circumstances: the number of people and mules, the quality of the provisions, the travelers' excellent appetites—everything, in short, down to the stumbling of the asses, is painstakingly recorded in the diary, for the education of the sedentary world.

It is with this principle in mind that I have decided to talk about my dear *Rosine,* an endearing animal that I love with true affection, and to devote an entire chapter to her.

In the six years that we have lived together, there has never been the slightest cooling in our fondness for each other; and if a few minor altercations have arisen between us, I must confess that I have always been the one more at fault, and that *Rosine* has always taken the first steps toward reconciliation.

In the evening, when she has been scolded, she retires gloomily and without a sound; the following day, at sunrise, she is at my bedside in an attitude of respect, and at the slightest movement from her master, at the first sign of waking, she announces her presence with the rapid thumping of her tail against my night table.

How could I ever deny affection to this tender creature that has never ceased loving me since the day we began living together? It would be beyond my memory's power to enumerate all the people who once took an interest in me only to forget me. I have had a few friends, several mistresses, a host of affairs, and even more acquaintances—but now I am nothing to all these people, who have forgotten even my name.

All those declarations, those offers of services! Oh, I could count on them, on their fortunes, on their eternal, unconditional friendship!

My dear *Rosine,* who has never offered me any service, has done me the greatest service that can be rendered to humanity: she has loved me before, and she still loves me now. Moreover—and I am not afraid to say it—I love her with a bit of the same sentiment that I accord my friends.—Say of it what you will.

CHAPTER XVIII

We left *Joanetti* in a state of astonishment, standing motionless before me, awaiting the end of the lofty explanation I had begun.

When he saw me suddenly bury my head in my dressing gown and end my explanation in that manner, he did not doubt for a moment that I had stopped short for want of good arguments, and that he had, therefore, discomfited me with the problem that he had set before me.

Despite the advantage he thus gained over me, he felt not the slightest hint of pride, and made no attempt to profit from this ascendancy.—After a brief moment of silence, he took the portrait, returned it to its place, and withdrew lightly on tiptoe.—He was keenly aware that his presence was a sort of humiliation for me, and his sense of tact told him he should withdraw, without my noticing.—His behavior on this occasion impressed me greatly and brought him forever closer to my heart. No doubt he will also find a place in the reader's heart; and if, after reading the chapter to follow, there is anyone so insensitive to deny him that, then heaven must have given him a heart of stone.

CHAPTER XIX

"Good Lord.!" I said to him one day, "this is the third time I've had to tell you to buy me a brush. What a blockhead! What a brute!"—He answered not a word; indeed, he had said nothing in response to a similar outburst the day before. He is so conscientious, I didn't know what to make of it.—"Go find a cloth to clean my shoes," I said to him angrily. As he went, I regretted having been so sharp with him. And my ire vanished entirely when I saw how carefully he tried to avoid touching my stockings while wiping the dust from my shoes. I put my hand on his shoulder as a gesture of reconciliation. "Could it be," I thought to myself at that moment, "that there are men who clean others' shoes for money?"—That word *money* was a sudden illumination for me. At once I remembered that it had been a long time since I had given any to my manservant.—*"Joanetti,"* I said, withdrawing my foot, "have you any money?" At this question, a half-smile of vindication appeared on his lips.—"No, Monsieur, it's eight days now that I haven't a sou; I spent everything I had on your purchases." — "And the brush? . . . Is that why?" He smiled again;—whereas he could have told his master: "No, I am not a blockhead, a *brute,* as you so cruelly called your faithful servant. Pay me the 23 francs, 10 sous, and 4 deniers that you owe me, and I shall buy you your brush." He let himself be mistreated rather than expose his master to embarrassment.

God bless him! Philosophers! Christians! Did you read that?

"Here, *Joanetti,*" I said to him. "Here, go and buy the brush."

"But, Monsieur, do you wish to remain with one white shoe and one black shoe?"

"Go, I say, and buy the brush. Never mind the dust on my shoe."

He went out. I took the cloth and with great pleasure cleaned my left shoe, upon which I let fall a tear of repentance.

CHAPTER XX

The walls of my room are hung with prints and paintings that greatly embellish it. I most sincerely wish I could let the reader examine them one by one, to amuse and distract him along the road that remains to be traveled before we reach my writing desk; but it is as impossible to explain a painting clearly as it is to paint a faithful portrait on the basis of a description.

What excitement the reader would feel, for example, in contemplating the first print to come before his eyes!—In it he would see the unhappy *Charlotte* slowly wiping, with trembling hand, *Albert's* pistols.*—Dark forebodings, and all the pangs of love without hope or consolation, are etched in her face, while the cold *Albert,* surrounded by his bags of legal briefs and old papers of every sort, icily turns about to wish his friend a pleasant voyage. How many times have I been tempted to break the glass covering this print, to tear *Albert* away from his table, to tear him to pieces in fact, and trample him underfoot!—But there will always be too many *Alberts* in this world. What sensitive man does not have his own, with whom he is forced to live and against whom the outpourings of the soul, the tender emotions of the heart, the flights of the fancy break like waves against the rocks?—Happy is the man who can find a friend whose heart and mind are right for him; a friend who will join with him in a commonality of taste, sentiment, and knowledge; a friend who is not tormented by ambition or self-interest—who prefers the shade of a tree to the pomp of a court.—Happy is the man who has a friend!

CHAPTER XXI

I used to have one. Death took him from me, cut him down in his first flower, at the moment when his friendship had become a pressing need for me. We gave each other strength during the arduous travails of war; we shared a single pipe between us; we drank

33

from the same cup; we slept under the same tent, and in the unfortunate circumstances in which we found ourselves, the place where we lived together became our new home. I saw him exposed to all the perils of war, a disastrous war. Death seemed to spare us each for the other; it took aim at him a thousand times without ever hitting the mark, but this was only to make his loss more painful to me. Had the clash of arms, the excitement that overwhelms one's soul in the presence of danger, prevented his cries from reaching my heart, had his death been useful to his country and detrimental to the enemy, I should have regretted it less;—but to lose him amid the pleasures of winter quarters! To see him die in my arms when he looked to be bursting with health, at a moment when our bonds were growing stronger in an atmosphere of rest and tranquility!—Alas! I shall never get over it. Yet in my heart alone does his memory survive; it has vanished for those among whom he lived, and who have replaced him in their hearts. This thought makes the pain of his loss all the greater for me. Nature, likewise indifferent to the fate of individuals, dons anew her bright spring dress, adorns herself in all her beauty round the cemetery where he lies. The trees cover themselves in leaves and twine their branches; birds sing amid the foliage; bees hum among the flowers; everything breathes joy and life in death's abode.—And in the evening, as the moon shines in the sky and I meditate not far from that sad place, I hear the cricket gaily carry on its tireless song, hidden in the grass covering my friend's silent grave. The senseless destruction of living things and all the sorrows of humanity count for nothing in the great whole.—The death of a sensitive man expiring in the company of his disconsolate friends, and that of a butterfly cut down by the chill morning air inside the calyx of a flower, are similar moments in the course of nature. Man is nothing but a phantom, a shadow, a mist that scatters in air.

But the glow of daybreak now begins to brighten the sky; the dark thoughts troubling me vanish with the night, and hope is reborn in my heart.—No, he who thus floods the East with light does not make it shine in my eyes only to plunge me shortly into the night of nothingness. He who laid out this boundless horizon, who raised these enormous masses of stone, whose sun begilds the icy summits, also commanded my heart to beat and my mind to think.

No, my friend did not pass into nothingness; no matter what barrier may separate us, I will see him again.—But it's not on a syllogism that I base my hopes.—The flight of an insect through the air is enough to convince me; and often the sight of the countryside, the sweet scent of the wind, and I know not what spell inhabiting the air about me, raise my thoughts so high that irrefutable proof of immortality forcefully enters my soul and fills it wholly.

CHAPTER XXII

The chapter I have just written had long been offering itself to my pen, and I had repeatedly turned it away. I had promised myself to show only my soul's smiling face in this book; but this resolution, like so many others, has eluded me. I hope the sensitive reader will forgive me for having requested a few tears of him; yet if anyone finds that, *in all truth,** I could have omitted that sorrowful passage, he may tear it out of his copy, or even toss the whole book into the fire.—

It is enough for me that you, my dear *Jenny,* should find it to be after your own heart, you, the best and most beloved of women;—you, the best and most beloved of sisters. To you I dedicate this book. If it wins your approval, it cannot fail to win that of all sensitive and delicate hearts; and if you will forgive me the follies that occasionally escape from my pen against my better judgment, I shall brave all the censors in the world.*

Chapter XXIII

I will say only one word about the next print. It shows the family of the wretched *Ugolino,** perishing of hunger. Around him, one of his sons lies motionless at his feet; the others are holding out their enfeebled arms to him, asking him for bread, while the wretched father, leaning against a column of the prison, his eyes fixed and wild, his face immobile—in the horrible tranquility granted by the final moments of despair—dies at once his own death and that of all his children, enduring all that human nature can endure.

Brave Chevalier d'*Assas!* There you are, perishing under a hundred bayonets, for an act of bravery, a heroism no longer known today.*

And you who weep under those palm trees, unhappy negress! you whom a barbarian, surely not an Englishman, has betrayed and abandoned—what am I saying?—you whom he had the cruelty to sell as a lowly slave, despite your love and devotion, despite the fruit of his tenderness that you carried in your womb;—I will not pass before your image without paying due homage to your sensitivity and your sorrow.

Let us pause for a moment before this next painting: here a young shepherdess is tending her flock all alone at the summit of the Alps: she is sitting on an old, fallen pine trunk whitened by many winters; her feet are covered by the large leaves of a clump of *cacalia,* whose lily flower rises up above her head. Lavender, thyme, anemones, and centaurea, flowers of every species that we take pains to cultivate in our hothouses and gardens, which grow in the Alps in all their primitive beauty, make up the bright carpet on which her sheep roam.—Gentle shepherdess, tell me, where is this charming corner of earth that you inhabit? From what distant sheepfold did you set out this morning at daybreak?—Might I come and live there with you?—But, alas! the sweet tranquility you enjoy will vanish before long: the demon of war, not content with devastating cities, will soon bring strife and terror even to your solitary retreat. Already the soldiers are advancing; I can see them scaling mountain upon mountain, coming closer and closer to the clouds.—The cannon blast resounds in thunder's lofty abode. Flee, shepherdess, hie with your flock; take refuge in the most secluded caverns of your wilderness; there is no more peace on this unhappy earth.

CHAPTER XXIV

I do not know how it happens, but for some time now my chapters all end on an ominous note. In vain I fix my gaze, at the start of each, on some agreeable object;—in vain I set sail in calm waters, only to meet with a squall which sets me adrift.—To put an end to these disturbances, which leave me unable to master my thoughts, and to pacify my racing heart, which so many touching images have overly excited, I see no other remedy than to give a disquisition.— Yes, I wish to put such a block of ice on my heart.

And this disquisition will be on painting, for to

discuss any other subject would be impossible. I cannot come all the way down from the point to which I had ascended just a moment ago: it is, moreover, my uncle *Toby's Hobby-Horse*.*

I should like, in passing, to say a few words on the question of whether the enchanting art of painting is superior to that of music, or vice versa: yes, I wish to throw something into the scale, be it but a grain of sand, even an atom.

In the painter's favor, it is said that he leaves something behind him; his paintings survive him and immortalize his memory.

It is countered that composers of music also leave behind their operas and concertos:—but music is subject to the whims of fashion; painting is not.— The pieces of music that so touched our forebears sound ridiculous to today's enthusiasts, and they are classed with the comic operas, to elicit laughter from the grandchildren of those whom they once moved to tears.

The paintings of Raphael will enchant our descendants just as they delighted our ancestors.

And that is my grain of sand.

"What does it matter to me," said Madame de *Hautcastel* to me one day, "whether the music of *Cherubini* or *Cimarosa* differs from that of their predecessors?—What does it matter to me whether old music makes me laugh, if the new music stirs me so delightfully? Is it necessary for my happiness that my pleasures should resemble those of my great-great-grandmother? Why do you talk to me about painting, an art that is enjoyed only by a very restricted class of people, when music enchants everything that breathes?"

I have little idea, at present, how one might respond to this observation, which I hardly expected when beginning this chapter.

Had I foreseen it, perhaps I should not have undertaken this disquisition. And let no one take this for a musician's trick.—On my honor, I am not a musician;—no, I am not, as heaven, and all those who have heard me play the violin, are my witnesses.

Yet supposing the merit of the one art to be equal to the other, one ought not be too hasty in inferring the merit of the art from that of the artist.—We have seen children play the harpsichord like great masters, but we have never seen a twelve-year-old who was a good painter. Painting, beyond taste and feeling, requires a thoughtful mind, which musicians can do without. Every day we see thoughtless, heartless men draw bewitching sounds from a violin or harp.

The human animal can be trained to play the harpsichord, and when he is trained by a good teacher, the soul can travel at leisure while the fingers proceed mechanically to evoke sounds in which it has no part whatsoever.—On the other hand, one cannot paint even the simplest thing in the world without the soul's employing all its faculties.

If, however, somebody took it upon himself to distinguish between the music of composition and that of performance, I must confess that I should be a little perplexed for it.—Alas! if all writers of disquisitions acted in good faith, all their efforts would end this way.—For when beginning the investigation of a question, one usually assumes a dogmatic tone, because one has already secretly made up one's mind, just as I had done, in fact, in favor of painting, despite my hypocritical impartiality; but discussion elicits objection,—and all ends up in doubt.

CHAPTER XXVI

Now that I am calmer, I shall attempt to speak dispassionately about the two portraits that follow the painting of the Alpine shepherdess.

Raphael! Your portrait could not have been painted by any other than you. Who else would have dared attempt it?—Your open face, sensitive and thoughtful, bespeaks your character and genius.

To please your ghost, next to you I have placed the portrait of your mistress, whom all men of all ages will forever call to account for the sublime works of which the arts have been deprived by your premature death.

As I contemplate Raphael's portrait I feel overwhelmed with a nearly religious respect for this great man who in the prime of his life had already surpassed all the ancients, and whose paintings fill modern artists with admiration and despair.—My soul, in admiring him, feels a surge of indignation at that Italian woman who preferred her love to her lover, and who extinguished the celestial fire, the divine genius, in his breast.*

Wretched woman! Did you not know that Raphael had promised a painting greater than the *Transfiguration*?—Were you not aware that in your arms you held nature's darling, the father of rapture, a sublime genius—a god?

As my soul was making these observations, her *companion,* casting an attentive eye upon the ravishing face of that deadly beauty, felt quite ready to forgive her for the death of Raphael.

In vain my soul chided the *other* for this foolish weakness; her reproaches fell on deaf ears.— Between these two Beings, on such occasions as this, a curious dialogue develops, which too often ends up to the advantage of the *lesser principle.*—I shall reserve a sampling of this for a later chapter.

If, for example, my soul did not abruptly break off the discussion at that moment,—if she granted the *other* the leisure to contemplate the well-rounded, graceful forms of the lovely Roman lady, intelligence would ignominiously lose its ascendancy.

And if, at this critical moment, I were suddenly granted the privilege accorded *Pygmalion,*—without possessing the slightest spark of the genius that makes Raphael's aberrations forgivable,—I should be capable—capable indeed—of dying the same death as he.*

CHAPTER XXVII

The prints and paintings of which I have just spoken pale and cease to exist the moment one sets one's eyes on the picture that follows; indeed the immortal works of *Raphael, Correggio,* and the entire Italian school suffer from the comparison. I always save it for last, as the *pièce de réserve,* whenever I grant some interested wayfarer the pleasure of traveling with me; and I assure you that ever since I have been showing this sublime image to connoisseurs and illiterates, to sophisticates, artisans, women, children, and even to animals, I have always seen the spectators show, each in his own way, signs of pleasure and astonishment, so admirably is nature rendered in it.

Well, what image could one present to you, Gentlemen, what spectacle could one place before your eyes, Ladies, that would be more certain to win your approval than a faithful representation of yourselves? The image of which I speak is a mirror's reflection, and as yet nobody has ever dared criticize it. It is, for all those who look at it, a perfect image to which none can take exception.

You will, no doubt, agree that it must be counted as one of the marvels of the country I am traveling through.

I'll not dwell on the pleasure the natural scientist takes in pondering light's strange marvels as it reproduces every thing in nature on that polished surface. To the sedentary traveler, the mirror offers a thousand alluring reflections, a thousand observations, and this makes it a useful, precious object.

You whom Love has held or still holds in thrall, be advised that it is in front of a mirror that he whets his arrows and plots his cruelties; there he rehearses his maneuvers, studies his movements, preparing himself in advance for the war he is about to declare; there he practices his tender glances, his sweet little gestures and cunning sulks, just as an actor practices in front of his own likeness before going out to face the public.

Always impartial, of course, a mirror gives back to the onlooker the rosiness of youth or the wrinkles of age, never slandering or flattering anyone.—

44

Unique among the counselors to the powerful, it always tells the truth.

This advantage once made me wish I had a moral mirror, in which all might see themselves with all their vices and virtues. I even dreamed of offering a prize to any Academy that could devise such an invention, when after long reflection I realized how useless it would have been.

Very rarely, alas, does ugliness recognize itself and break the glass! In vain do mirrors multiply all around us, reflecting light and reality with geometrical precision: the moment the rays penetrate our eyes and portray us as we really are, vanity slips its deceitful prism between us and our image and shows us a god.

And of all the prisms that have existed since the first one emerged from the hands of the immortal Newton, none has possessed so great a force of refraction or produced colors so lovely and bright as the prism of our vanity.

Now, since ordinary mirrors proclaim the truth in vain, and everyone remains pleased with his appearance,—since they fail to make people acknowledge their physical imperfections, what would be the use of a moral mirror? Few would cast so much as a glance at it, and none would recognize himself in it.—Philosophers alone would waste their time looking at themselves.—And I even have my doubts of that.

In seeing the mirror for what it is, I hope nobody will blame me for having ranked it above all the paintings of the Italian school. The Ladies, whose preferences are never wrong, and whose determination ought to settle this question, customarily cast their first glance at this image upon entering an apartment. Countless times at balls have I seen Ladies, and even Ladies' Men, forget their lovers, mistresses, the dance, and all the other pleasures of the occasion, to contemplate, with manifest satisfaction, that spellbinding image—and even honor it from time to time with a furtive glance in the midst of the most spirited quadrille.

Who, therefore, could possibly object to my ranking it with the masterpieces of the art of *Apelles?**

CHAPTER XXVIII

I had at last arrived at a point very near my writing table, and already could have touched, by extending my arm, the corner nearest me, when I found myself on the verge of destroying the fruit of all my labors and losing my very life.—I really ought to leave the accident that befell me unmentioned, so as not to discourage others from travel, but it is so difficult to fall from the post-chaise that I am using, you will be compelled to admit one must be unlucky in the extreme—as indeed I am—to encounter such danger.

I found myself laid out on the floor, utterly up-ended, and it happened so quickly, so unexpectedly, that I should have doubted the occurrence of the accident itself had a ringing in my head, and a sharp pain in my left shoulder, not verified its authenticity all too clearly.

It was yet another naughty trick of *my other half*.—Startled by the voice of a pauper suddenly begging for alms at my door, and by *Rosine*'s barking, the beast turned my armchair brusquely about, before my soul had the time to notice that a brick was missing behind it, and the force of it was so violent that my post chaise lurched fully outside its center of gravity and capsized on top of me.

This, I must admit, is one of those occasions where my greatest complaint is with my soul; for instead of getting angry at her own momentary truancy and scolding her companion for his reckless haste, she so forgot herself that she partook of a most *animal* resentment and abused, with words, that poor innocent at the door. *"Good-for-nothing!"* she shouted at him. (An abominable reproach, invented by avaricious, cruel wealth!)—*"Monsieur,"* he said, to move me to pity, *"I am from Chambéry."*—"Too bad for you."—*"My name is Jacques; I'm the man you saw in the country;—it was I who was taking the sheep to pasture."*—"What are you doing here?"—My soul was beginning to regret the brutality of her initial words.—I even think she regretted them an instant before blurting them out. As

47

when suddenly coming upon a ditch or a mudhole along the road, one may see it, but one hasn't enough time to avoid it.

It was *Rosine* who made me see reason and repent: she had recognized *Jacques,* who had often shared his bread with her, and through her friendliness expressed her gratitude and remembrance.

Meanwhile *Joanetti,* who had gathered the leavings of my meal, which were destined for him, gave them without hesitation to *Jacques.*

Poor *Joanetti!*

Thus, in my travels, am I taking lessons in philosophy and humanity from my valet and my dog.

CHAPTER XXIX

Before going any further, I wish to dispel a doubt that may have entered the minds of my readers.

I should not want, for anything in the world, to be suspected of having embarked on this voyage because I didn't know what else to do and was forced, in one way or another, by circumstances: I can assure you, and I swear by all that is dear to me, that I had planned to undertake such a voyage long before the event that deprived me of my freedom for forty-two days. This forced retreat was simply an opportunity to set out a bit sooner.

I know that the unsolicited declaration I have just

made will appear suspect to some;—yet I also know that suspicious people will not read this book;—they have enough to keep themselves busy at home and among their friends: they have other matters to attend to.—Good people will believe me.

I do admit, however, that I would rather have undertaken my voyage at another time and chosen, as the proper moment, Lent instead of Carnival. Nevertheless, certain philosophical reflections, which have come to me from above, have greatly helped me to endure being deprived of the host of pleasures that Turin has to offer at this time of boisterous excitement.—There is no doubt, I said to myself, that the walls of my room are not so magnificently adorned as those of a ballroom: the silence of my *cabin* hardly compares to the delightful din of music and dancing. Still, among the radiant figures one encounters at such balls, there are certainly some more bored than I.

And why should I concern myself with those who are in a more agreeable situation than my own, when the world is teeming with people more wretched than I?—Rather than flee in my imagination to that *casino* where all those beauties are yet eclipsed by the young *Eugénie,* to appreciate how fortunate I am I need only stop a moment along one of the streets that lead to it.—A heap of sorry wretches, huddled half-naked under the porticoes of those sumptuous apartments, look about to die of cold and hardship.— What a sight! I should like this page of my book to be known throughout the world; I should like all to know that in this city where everything breathes opulence, a crowd of paupers, on the coldest winter nights, sleep out in the open, heads resting against a cornerstone or on the doorstep of a palace.

Here it's a group of children, pressed against one another so as not to freeze to death.—There, a woman trembling, with no voice to express her grievance.—Passers-by come and go, unmoved by a spectacle to which they have grown accustomed.— The noise of the carriages, the voice of intemperance, and the spellbinding sounds of music mingle at times with the cries of these wretches, creating a frightful dissonance.

CHAPTER XXX

Those who would rush to pass judgment on a city on the basis of the preceding chapter would be quite mistaken. I spoke of the poor that one finds there, of their pitiful cries and the indifference of certain people to their plight; but I said nothing of the multitude of charitable men who sleep while the others have fun, then rise at daybreak and go out to help the unfortunate, without witnesses and without ostentation.—No, I will not keep silent on this matter: I will write it on the back of this page, *which all the world should read*.

After having thus shared their good fortune with

their brothers, after having poured balm upon those pain-battered hearts, they go into the churches, while weary vice sleeps on eiderdown, and offer their prayers up to God, thanking him for his goodness: while the light of a solitary lamp in the temple still contends with that of the dawning day, they are already prostrate before the altars;—and the Eternal Father, irritated by man's cruelty and greed, holds his thunderbolt in hand, ready to strike.

CHAPTER XXXI

I wanted to say something about those unfortunate people during my voyage, because the thought of their misery has often distracted me along the road. Several times, struck by the difference between their situation and my own, I have stopped my coach at once, and my room has suddenly seemed prodigiously lavish. What useless luxury! Six chairs, two tables, a writing desk, a mirror! What ostentation! My bed especially: my pink-and-white bed, with its two mattresses, seemed to outdo the monarchs of the East in magnificence and voluptuousness.—Such reflections made me indifferent to the pleasures that had been forbidden me. And after reflection upon reflection, my outburst of philosophy became so great that, had I seen a ball in the neighboring room, had I heard the sounds of violins and clarinets, I should not have stirred from my place;—I could have heard with my own ears the melodious voice of *Marchesini,* a voice that has often transported me outside myself, and still I should not have moved;— even more than this, I could have gazed upon the most beautiful woman in Turin, *Eugénie* herself, decked out from head to toe by Mme *Repous,** and felt nothing at all.—That, however, is not a good thing.

CHAPTER XXXII

But allow me, Gentlemen, to ask you a question: Do you enjoy yourselves as much as you used to at a ball or at the theatre?—For my part, I must say that for some time now, any large gathering of people inspires a kind of terror in me.—I am, in such circumstances, assailed by a sinister dream.—Try as I might to banish it from my mind, it always comes back, like *Athaliah*'s dream.* This is perhaps because the soul, now inundated with so many dark ideas and heartrending spectacles, everywhere finds causes for sorrow;—like a tainted stomach that turns even the most wholesome foods to poison.—Be that as it may, my dream is as follows: When I am at one of those balls, amidst that crowd of amiable, handsome people dancing and singing—people who weep at tragedies, who express only joy, candor, and cordiality—I say to myself:—What if suddenly a white bear, a philosopher, a tiger, or some other animal of that sort were to join this polite gathering, go up to the orchestra, and shout out madly: "Wretched humans! Harken to the truth that speaks through me: you are oppressed and tyrannized; you are unhappy; you are bored.—Rouse yourselves from your sleep.

"You, musicians, begin by smashing your instruments over your heads; let each man arm himself with a dagger; think no more of entertainment, of parties; go up into the boxes and slit everyone's throat; and let the women also soak their timid hands in blood.

"Go now, you are *free,* wrest your king from his throne and your God from his sanctuary."

—Well! how many of these *charming* people would carry out what the tiger said?—How many were perhaps already thinking about it before he entered? Who knows?—Were they not dancing in Paris five years ago?*

"Joanetti! Shut all the doors and windows.—I no longer wish to see the light of day; let no man enter my room;—place my sabre within my reach;—you too, leave, and never show your face again."

Chapter XXXIII

"No, no, please stay, *Joanetti*, stay, poor boy—
and you too, dear *Rosine;* you who can sense my
troubles and allay them with your affections, come,
Rosine, come to your letter V and rest."

Chapter XXXIV

The fall from my post-chaise has done the reader
the favor of shortening my voyage by a good dozen
chapters, since while picking myself up I found myself right in front of my writing desk, having missed
my chance to comment upon a number of prints and
paintings still remaining to be examined, which
might have prolonged my digressions on art.

Leaving behind, then, on the right, the portraits of
Raphael and his mistress, the Chevalier d'*Assas* and
the *Alpine shepherdess,* and moving leftward along
the wall toward the window, we come to my desk:
it's the first and most visible object to meet the traveler's eyes, if he follows the route I have just indicated.

Above the desk are some shelves that serve as a
library;—the whole is crowned by a bust at the top of
the pyramid, which embellishes the landscape more
than any other object.

Pulling open the first drawer on the right, we find an inkstand, paper of every kind, an assortment of quills, all cut, and sealing wax.—All this would make even the most indolent person inclined to start writing.—I am certain, my dear *Jenny,* that if you chanced to open this drawer, you would answer the letter I wrote to you last year.—In the corresponding drawer on the left, there lies in a confused heap the material of the touching story of the fair captive of Pignerol, which you shall soon read, dear friends.*

Between these two drawers there is a hollow in which I toss my letters as I receive them. There you will find every letter I have received in the last ten years; the oldest are arranged in several packets according to their dates; the new ones are all jumbled together. I even have several from my early youth.

What a pleasure it is to revisit in those letters the charming circumstances of our early years! To be transported anew to those happy times that we shall never see again!

Alas! How heavy my heart is, how sorrowfully it delights as my eyes glance over lines composed by a person who no longer exists! Look at those characters: it was his heart that guided his hand; I am the one for whom he wrote this letter—and it is all that I have left of him.

When I put my hand inside that nook, rarely do I escape before the end of the day. Thus does the traveler pass quickly through a few Italian provinces, look at a few things in haste and superficially, only to settle in Rome for months at a time.—I work the mine's richest vein: how my ideas have changed, and my feelings too! How different my friends are, when I look at them then and now! I see them madly driven by schemes that no longer move them at all! There was one event that we considered a great calamity—but the end of the letter is missing, and the event has been competely forgotten. I shall never know what it was.—We were besieged by a thousand preconceptions: we knew nothing of the world or the people in it; but on the other hand, what fervor in our intercourse! What intimate ties! What boundless confidence!

We were happy in our mistakes.—And now, alas! that is no longer the case; we too, like everyone else, have had to read the human heart;—and the truth, falling among us like a bomb, has forever destroyed the enchanted palace of illusion.

CHAPTER XXXV

I could readily write a chapter on the withered rose I have before me, were the subject worth the trouble: it's a flower from last year's carnival. I picked it myself in one of the *Valentino* hothouses; and that same evening, an hour before the ball, full of hope and in pleasant spirits, I went to offer it to Mme de *Hautcastel*. She took it,—set it on her dressing table without looking at it, and without even looking at me.—But how could she ever notice me, when she was so busy looking at herself? Standing before a tall mirror, her hair all dressed, she was putting the last touches on her toilette; indeed so preoccupied was she, her attention so utterly absorbed in the ribbons, veils, and finery of every sort piled up before her, that I received not even a glance or a sign.—I resigned myself: humbly, I held out a ready assortment of pins in my hand; but since her pin cushion was within easier reach, she took her pins from there;— if I extended my hand, she did take them, indifferently, from there as well, though groping about, never removing her eyes from the mirror, lest she should lose sight of herself.

For a time I held a second mirror in front of her, so she could better judge her appearance; and as her figure was reflected back and forth from one mirror to the other, I saw at that moment an infinite perspective of coquettes, none of which paid any attention to me. In short, shall I say it?—we were a sorry sight, my rose and I.

In the end I lost patience and, unable any longer to resist the resentment eating away at me, I set down the mirror and exited angrily, without saying goodbye.

"Are you leaving?" she said to me, turning to the side to look at her waist in profile.—I did not answer, but listened a few moments at the door to see what sort of effect my abrupt departure would have.—*"Can't you see,"* she said to her maid after a moment of silence, *"can't you see that this* caraco *is*

much too wide, and that we need to make a tuck with pins?''

How and why this withered rose happens to be on a shelf over my desk, I certainly shall never tell, for I said that a withered rose did not merit a chapter.

Note well, Ladies: I have ventured no comment whatsoever on the adventure of the withered rose. I have not said that Mme de *Hautcastel* was right or wrong to prefer her finery to me, nor that I was entitled to being received in any other manner.

I am even more careful not to draw any general conclusions as to the reality, the intensity, and the duration of the affections of Ladies for their friends. I shall limit myself to sending this chapter (since it is, after all, a chapter)—to sending it, I say, out into the world with the rest of the voyage, without addressing it, or recommending it, to anyone.

I shall add only a bit of advice for you, Gentlemen: Never forget that on the day of a ball, your mistress is no longer yours.

The moment the dressing begins, the lover becomes nothing more than a husband: the ball alone is the lover.

Everyone knows, moreover, that a husband has nothing to gain by trying to make his wife love him by force. Therefore, bear your hurt patiently, and with a smile.

And also, Monsieur, have no illusions: if she shows great delight in seeing you at the ball, it is not as a lover that you give such pleasure, for you are a husband: it is because you are part of the ball, and because you are, therefore, a fraction of her new conquest, a *decimal* of a lover:—or else it is because you dance well, and you will therefore make her shine: lastly, the only flattering thing there might be for you in her warm reception is that in claiming a man of quality like you as her lover, she hopes to stir the jealousy of her friends; without this consideration, she would not even look at you.

There is no question, then, but that you must resign yourself and wait until your role as husband is over.—I know more than one man who would gladly be discharged of it at so fair a price.

CHAPTER XXXVI

I promised a dialogue between my soul and the *other;* but certain chapters elude me, or rather, other chapters flow from my pen as though against my will and throw my plans off course: among this number is the one about my library, which I will make as brief as possible.—The forty-two days are going to come to an end, and not even that entire length of time would suffice to complete the description of the rich country through which I am traveling with such pleasure.

My library, then, is made up of novels, if you must know;—yes, of novels, and a few choice poets.

As if I didn't have enough troubles of my own, I

willingly share those of a thousand imaginary characters as well, and feel them as keenly as I do mine: how many tears have I not shed for the unhappy *Clarissa* and for *Charlotte*'s lover?*

Yet if I thus seek out fictitious woes, in compensation I find in this imaginary world a virtue, goodness, and unselfishness which I have yet to encounter thus combined in the real world I inhabit.—In a book I find a woman according to my desires: free of moods, whims, deceit;—to say nothing of her beauty: my imagination takes care of that; I make her so beautiful that one can find no fault whatsoever with her; then, closing the book, which no longer measures up to my thoughts, I take her by the hand and we roam through a land a thousand times lovelier than Eden. What painter could ever depict the enchanted landscape in which I have placed the goddess of my dreams? What poet could ever describe the keen and diverse sensations I experience in those enchanted realms?

How many times have I cursed that Mr. *Cleveland*,* who at every moment is embarking upon new misfortunes that he could have avoided!—I cannot bear this book and its chain of calamities; yet if I open it inadvertently, then I must devour it to the very end.

How could I leave the poor man among the *Abaquis?* What would become of him at the hands of those savages? Even less do I dare abandon him on the excursion he takes to escape his captivity.

In short, I share his afflictions so intensely, become so concerned with him and his unfortunate family, that the sudden appearance of the fierce *Ruintons* makes my hair stand on end; a cold sweat comes over me as I read this passage, and my terror is as keen and real as if I myself were to be roasted and eaten by that wicked lot.

When, on the other hand, I have had enough of weeping and wooing, I seek out some poet and depart anew for another world.

CHAPTER XXXVII

From the expedition of the Argonauts to the Assembly of Notables;* from the very bottom of Hell to the last fixed star beyond the Milky Way, to the limits of the universe, to the very portals of chaos—such is the vast field I wander, lengthwise and breadthwise and entirely at my leisure, since I have as much time as space at my disposal.—And there I transport my existence, after Homer, Milton, Virgil, Ossian, etc.

Every event that has taken place between those two eras; every country, every world, and every being that has existed between those two times—they are all mine; they belong to me every bit as much, and as legitimately, as the vessels that entered the port of *Piraeus* belonged to a certain Athenian.

I especially love those poets who transport me

back to earliest antiquity: the death of the ambitious Agamemnon, the furies of Orestes, the whole tragic story of the house of Atreus, persecuted by the heavens, inspire a terror in me that modern events could never provoke.

Witness the fateful urn containing Orestes' ashes. Who would not shudder at such a sight? Electra! unhappy sister, set your mind at rest; Orestes himself brings the urn; the ashes are those of his enemies.

One no longer finds riverbanks comparable to those of the *Xanthus* or the *Scamander;*—one no longer sees plains like those of *Hesperia* or *Arcadia.* Where are the isles of *Lemnos* and *Crete* today? Where is the famous labyrinth? Where is the rock that the forsaken *Ariadne* bedewed with her tears?— One no longer encounters the like of *Theseus,* much less of *Hercules;* the men of today, even the heroes, are pygmies.

Then, when I wish to afford myself a view of divine inspiration and to delight in all the powers of my imagination, I cling fearlessly to the flowing robe of Albion's sublime blind poet as he prepares to soar heavenward and dares to approach the throne of the Eternal.—What Muse could have sustained him at such a lofty height, whither no man before him had ever dared lift his eyes?—And from Heaven's dazzling vault upon which *Mammon* gazed with eyes of envy, I descend, in horror, into the vast caverns of Satan's abode;—I take part in the Infernal Council; I join the crowd of rebellious spirits and listen to their speeches.—

But here I must confess to a weakness for which I have often reproached myself.

I cannot help but take a certain interest in this poor Satan, ever since he fell from heaven (Milton's Satan, that is). While I condemn the rebel spirit's obstinacy, still his steadfastness in the face of overwhelming adversity, and his great courage, compel my admiration in spite of myself;—though I am not unaware of the afflictions originating in his calamitous plot to break through the gates of hell to disturb the peace of our first parents' home, I could never wish, try as I might, to see him perish along the way, in the confusion of chaos. I even believe I would gladly lend him a hand, if not for the shame that holds me back. I follow his every movement and enjoy traveling with him as much as if I were in good company. No matter how much I might tell myself that he is, after all, a devil, that his purpose is the destruction of the human race, that he is a true democrat—not like those of Athens, but rather like those of Paris—, none of it avails in curing me of my predisposition in his favor.

What a tremendous scheme! And what daring in its execution!

When the vast, threefold gates of hell flew open before him, and the pit of night and the void yawned in all its horror at his feet, he ran his intrepid eye over chaos's dark empire and, without hesitation, spreading his tremendous wings, which could have covered a whole army, cast himself into the abyss.

I challenge the boldest among you to do the

same.—It is, in my opinion, one of the finest efforts of the imagination, and one of the greatest voyages ever taken—after the voyage around my room.

CHAPTER XXXVIII

Were I to attempt to describe even the most minuscule fraction of the noteworthy events that befall me when traveling about my library, I should never finish. *Cook*'s voyages, and the observations of his traveling companions, doctors *Banks* and *Solander,* are nothing compared to my adventures in this single region: also, I believe I should spend my entire life there in a kind of rapture if not for the bust I mentioned;—for my eyes and my thoughts always end up turning to it, no matter what the state of my soul may be; and when it is excessively troubled, or gives in to dejection, I have only to look at that bust to restore its natural equilibrium; it is the *tuning fork* according to which I adjust the variable and discordant assortment of sensations and perceptions that make up my existence.

What an excellent likeness!—There, indeed, one sees the features that nature gave to the most virtuous of men. Ah! if only the sculptor could have given visible shape to his superior soul, his genius, and his character!—But what am I getting into here? Is this the place to sing his praises? Is it to those around me that I address them? What do they care?

I shall limit myself to bowing before your cherished image, O peerless father! This image, alas! is all that I have left of you and my country; you departed this world just as iniquity was about to invade it; and so great are the evils with which it has overwhelmed us, that today the family cannot help but look upon your loss as a blessing. How many ills you would have known, had your life been longer! O my father!—Is the fate of your large family known to you in the abode of the blessed? Do you know that your children have been banished from the very country you served with such zeal and integrity for sixty years? Do you know that they are forbidden to visit your grave?—Yet tyranny could not take from them the most precious part of your heritage, the memory of your virtues, and the power of your example: amidst the torrent of crime that dragged their country and their fortune into the abyss, they remained unshakably united on the line that you had drawn for them. And when, one day, they can again bow down before your sacred remains, you shall recognize them still.*

CHAPTER XXXIX

I promised a dialogue, and I will keep my word.—
One morning, at daybreak, as the sun's rays were
gilding the peaks of Mount Viso and of the highest
mountains of the island at our antipodes,* *he* was
already awake, having been prematurely roused
either by the nocturnal visions that often put him in
an agitated state as fatiguing as it is useless, or by the
carnival that was then drawing to a close—this time
of pleasure and folly having an influence on the human organism comparable to that of phases of the
moon and the conjunction of certain planets.—In
short, *he* was awake, quite awake, in fact, when
my soul also decided to shake off the bonds of
sleep.

For a good while the latter had been sharing, in
confused fashion, the *other*'s sensations; yet she was
still entangled in sleep's veils, and these veils
seemed transformed into gauzes, fine linens, and
muslins.—Thus my poor soul was as though
wrapped up in all this finery, and the god of sleep, to
keep her more firmly in his sway, added tangled
blond braids, knotted ribbons, and pearl necklaces to
these bonds: and she looked a pitiable sight, to any
that might see her, thrashing about in that netting.

The agitation of the noblest part of myself was
imparted to the other, and then he, in turn, exerted
his own powerful influence upon my soul.—I had
fully reached a state difficult to describe, when my

soul, either by cleverness or by chance, suddenly discovered the way to free herself from the veils that were suffocating her. I do not know whether she found an opening or simply took it upon herself to remove them, which would have been more natural; in any event, she found her way out of the labyrinth. The tangled braids of hair were still there, but they were no longer an *obstacle;* they were, rather, a *means of escape:* my soul seized them as a drowning man fastens on to the grasses of the riverbank, but the pearl necklace broke in the process, and the pearls came unstrung, rolling onto the sofa and thence onto the parquet of Mme de *Hautcastel;*—for my soul, in an extravagance that would be difficult to explain, imagined she was at that Lady's home: a large bouquet of violets fell to the floor, and my soul, then waking, returned home, bringing reason and reality with her. As one may imagine, she strongly disapproved of all that had happened in her absence; and here begins the dialogue that is the subject of this chapter.

Never had my soul been made to feel so unwelcome. The accusations she took it upon herself to make at this critical moment succeeded in bringing discord to the household: it was a revolt, an outright insurrection.

"What is this!" said my soul. "So, when I'm away, instead of regaining your strength in restful sleep that you may better carry out my orders, you *insolently* (the term was a bit strong) decide to abandon yourself to raptures unsanctioned by my will?"

Unaccustomed to this haughty tone, the *other* re-joined angrily:

"How fitting, Madame (to prevent any sense of familiarity from entering the discussion), how fitting indeed that you should make such a show of decency and virtue. Ha! Are not your flights of fancy and your extravagant ideas the cause of all that you find disagreeable in me?—Eh, why were you not here?—Why should you have the right to enjoy yourself without me, all by yourself, on your frequent voyages?—Have I ever objected to your sojourns in the empyrean or in the Elysian Fields, your conversations with invisible intelligences, your profound speculations (a bit of mockery, as we can see), your castles in the air, your sublime systems?—So why, when you abandon me so, should I not also have the right to enjoy the benefits and pleasures that nature offers me?"

My soul, surprised by such spirit and eloquence, did not know what to reply.—To settle the matter, she attempted to cover in a veil of benevolence the reproaches to which she had just given vent; and to avoid the appearance of taking the first steps toward reconciliation, she likewise thought to assume a tone of ceremony.—"Monsieur," she said in turn, with affected cordiality.—If the reader found such formality out of place when addressed to my soul, what will he say now, though he may well have no wish to recall the subject of the dispute?—My soul had no idea of the utter ridiculousness of this manner of speaking, so thoroughly does passion obfuscate the intellect!—"Monsieur," she said, "I assure you that nothing would please me more than to see you enjoy all the pleasures of which your nature is capable, even when I may not share them, if these pleasures were not harmful to you and did not threaten the harmony that—" Here my soul was forcefully interrupted:—"No, no, I'll not be fooled by your pretended benevolence;—our compulsory stay in this room of our voyage, the wound I received, which nearly destroyed me, and which still bleeds,—are not all these things the fruit of your immoderate pride and your barbarous prejudices? My well-being, indeed, my very existence count for nothing when you are swept away by your passions—and you claim to care about me? And that your reproaches are dictated by our friendship?"

My soul saw clearly that she was not playing the better part on this occasion;—she was beginning, moreover, to realize that the heat of the dispute had effaced the cause, and so, taking advantage of the circumstance to create a diversion, "Go make some coffee," she said to *Joanetti,* as he entered the room. Once the tinkling of the cups attracted the *insurgent*'s full attention, he quickly forgot all the rest. In the same way, one shows a child a toy to make him forget the unwholesome fruit he demands with stamping feet.

I dozed off imperceptibly while the water heated up.—I was enjoying that charming pleasure I mentioned earlier to my readers, which one experiences when feeling oneself sleep. The delightful noise that

Joanetti made with the coffeepot against the andirons reverberated in my head, setting all my sensory fibers vibrating the way the striking of a harpstring sets the octaves resonating.—At last I saw a sort of shadow before me; I opened my eyes: it was *Joanetti.*—Ah! what a fragrance! what a lovely surprise! coffee! and cream! and a pyramid of toasted bread!—Good reader, do join me for breakfast.

Chapter XL

What a great wealth of delights good Mother Nature has bestowed upon people who in their hearts know how to enjoy life! And what variety in these delights! Who could ever count their innumerable shades of difference from one individual to the next, and in the different ages of life!—The blurred memory of those of my childhood still makes me quiver. Shall I attempt to describe those felt by a young man whose heart is beginning to burn with all the fires of sentiment? —At that happy age when one still knows nothing, not even the names, of self-interest, ambition, hatred, and all the shameful passions that debase and torment humanity; at that age—too brief, alas!—the sun shines with a brilliance that one will not see again for the rest of one's life. The air is purer, the fountains fresher, more limpid;—nature has aspects, woodlands have paths that one no longer finds in later years. Heavens! what fragrances the flowers exude! how delicious the fruit is! what colors paint the dawn!—All women are lovely and faithful; and men are good, kind, and sensitive. One encounters cordiality, sincerity, and unselfishness at every turn: in nature there are only flowers, virtues, and pleasures.

Do not love's turmoil and the hope of happiness flood our hearts with sensations as keen as they are diverse?—The spectacle of nature, its contemplation as a whole and in its details, affords the mind a vast, open field of delights. Then fancy, soaring over this ocean of pleasures, soon increases their number and intensity: different sensations unite and combine to form new ones: dreams of glory mingle with the palpitations of love: charity walks hand in hand with pride: and from time to time melancholy comes and casts its pall on us, turning our pleasures to tears.— In short, the mind's perceptions, the heart's sensations, the senses' very memory, are inexhaustible wellsprings of delight and happiness for man.— Be not surprised, therefore, that the noise which *Joanetti* made with the coffeepot against the andiron, and the unexpected appearance of a cup of cream, should have had so keen and pleasant an effect on me.

CHAPTER XLI

I donned at once my *traveling coat,* after examining it with a satisfied eye, and at that moment I
decided to do a chapter *ad hoc,* to acquaint the reader
with it. The form and use of such coats being rather
generally known, I shall speak more specifically of
their influence on the traveler's mind.—My winter
traveling coat is made of the warmest, most luxu-
rious fabric I could find: it covers me whole, from
head to toe; and when I am in my armchair, hands in
my pockets, head buried in the coat's collar, I resemble the footless, handless statue of *Vishnu* that one
sees in the temples of India.

One might object, perhaps, that the influence I
attribute to traveling coats is informed by prejudice;
what I can say for certain in this regard is that it
would seem to me as ridiculous to travel a single step
around my room, dressed in my uniform, with my
sword at my side, as it would to go out and into
society in my dressing gown.—When thus attired, in
full regimentals, not only would I not be up to con-
tinuing my voyage, but I believe I should not even be
capable of reading what I have written of it thus far,
much less of understanding it.

But does that surprise you? Do we not see people
every day who believe they are ill because they
haven't shaved or because someone else decides that
they look unwell and says so? Clothing has so great
an influence on men's minds that there are va-

letudinarians who feel much better when they see themselves in new clothes and a well-powdered wig; we see some who fool others and themselves in this way, by presenting a solid appearance;—then one fine morning they die with their hair all dressed, and their death shocks the world.

In short, among the class of men in whose midst I live, how many are there who, seeing themselves clad in a uniform, firmly believe themselves to be officers—until the sudden appearance of the enemy undeceives them?—Or worse still, if it pleases the king to allow one of them to add some embroidery to his dress, suddenly he thinks he's a general, and the whole army also gives him this title without laughing,—so great is clothing's influence on the human imagination.*

The following example will prove my point better still.

Sometimes we used to forget to give the Count de*** several days warning that it was his turn to mount guard;—a corporal would go wake him early in the morning of the very day he was supposed to serve, and give him this sad bit of news; yet the idea of rising at once, putting on his gaiters, and going out without having given any thought to it the night before so upset him that he preferred to send word that he was ill, and not to leave his quarters. He then put on his dressing gown and dismissed the hair-dresser; this made him look pale and sickly, and alarmed his wife and family.—And he did, indeed, feel *not quite right* on that day.

He said so to everyone, in part to keep up appearances, in part because he really believed that was how he felt.—Imperceptibly, the dressing gown exerted its influence; the broths he had drunk, willy-nilly, nauseated him; soon relatives and friends were inquiring after his health; that was more than enough to put him decidedly to bed.

In the evening, Doctor *Ranson** found his pulse to be somewhat *concentrated,* and ordered that he be bled the following day. Had his tour of duty lasted more than a month, that would have been the end of the patient.

Can there still be any doubt as to the influence of traveling coats on travelers, when one considers that the poor Count de*** nearly made the voyage to the next world for having put on his dressing gown at the wrong moment in this one?

CHAPTER XLII

I was sitting by the fire after dinner, wrapped in my *traveling coat* and deliberately open to all its influence, awaiting the moment of departure, when the vapors of digestion began to go to my head, so thoroughly blocking the passages through which ideas travel from the senses to the brain, that all communication was interrupted; and just as my senses ceased to transmit any idea whatsoever to my brain, so the latter in turn found itself unable to convey that electrical fluid that animates thought, the same with which the ingenious Doctor *Valli* resuscitates dead frogs.*

Having read this preamble, one will have little difficulty conceiving why my head fell onto my chest or how the muscles of the thumb and index finger of my right hand, being no longer quickened by that fluid, relaxed to the point that a volume of the marquis *Caraccioli,** which I was holding between that very thumb and finger, slipped out without my noticing and fell onto the hearthstone.

I had just had some visitors, and my conversation with these people had turned to the famous Doctor *Cigna,* who had just died, to the regret of all. He was scholarly, hard-working, a good physician and a famous botanist.*—As my thoughts dwelt on the merits of this resourceful man, I said to myself: "And yet, if I could call forth the souls of all those whom he may have dispatched to the other world, who knows whether his reputation might not suffer some damage?"

I had embarked unawares on a disquisition on medicine and the advances it has made since *Hippocrates.*—I wondered whether the famous figures of antiquity who died in their beds, such as *Pericles, Plato,* the celebrated *Aspasia,* and *Hippocrates* himself, had died like ordinary people, of worms, inflammations, or putrid fever, and had been bled and plied with endless cures.

It would be impossible to say exactly why I mused

upon these four personages instead of others.—Who can explain the reasons for a daydream?—All I can say is that it was my soul that called forth the doctors of Cos and Turin and the famous statesman who had done such wonderful things and made such great mistakes.

As for his lovely companion,* I humbly confess that it was the *other* who had called her to mind. When I think about it, however, I feel a tempting flutter of pride; for it is clear that in this daydream, the balance was four to one in favor of reason.—No small thing for a lieutenant.

Be that as it may, as I abandoned myself to these reflections, my eyes managed to shut and I fell into a deep sleep; yet as I closed my eyes, the images of the people I had been thinking of remained painted on that fine canvas that we call *memory,* and as these images mingled in my brain with the idea of the evocation of the dead, I soon saw arrive, one after another, *Hippocrates, Plato, Pericles, Aspasia,* and Doctor *Cigna* in his wig.

I saw them all sit down in the chairs still arranged around the fire; *Pericles* alone remained standing, to read the gazettes.

"If the discoveries you speak of were true," said *Hippocrates* to the doctor, "and if they were useful to medicine as you claim, I should see fewer souls descending each day into the shadowy realm; whereas their number, according to *Minos*'s registers, which I myself have checked, is consistently the same as it has always been."

Doctor *Cigna* turned to me: "You, no doubt, have heard mention of these discoveries," he said to me. "You must know of *Harvey*'s discovery of the circulation of the blood, and those of the immortal *Spallanzani* on digestion, the entire system of which is now common knowledge."*—And he gave a long summary of all the discoveries relating to medicine and of the host of cures for which we have chemistry to thank; and he crowned it all by giving a learned speech in favor of modern medicine.

"Am I to believe," I replied to him, "that these great men know nothing of what you have just told them, and that their souls, released from the shackles of matter, find all of nature somewhat obscure?"

"Ah, how mistaken you are!" exclaimed the *protophysician** of the Peloponnesus. "The mysteries of nature are concealed from the dead as from the living. Only he who created and rules all knows the great secret that men strive in vain to attain: that is the only sure thing we learn on the banks of the Styx. And take my advice," he said, turning to the doctor, "cast aside that remnant of *esprit de corps* that you have brought with you from the realm of the living. Since the labors of a thousand generations, and all the discoveries man has ever made, have not prolonged human life by so much as an instant, and since *Charon* each day ferries an equal number of shades in his bark, let us cease to trouble ourselves uselessly defending an art that, in the land of the dead where we are, would not be of any use even to

77

doctors.'' Thus spoke the celebrated *Hippocrates,* to my great astonishment.

Doctor *Cigna* smiled. And as ghosts could never turn a blind eye to the facts, nor silence the truth, not only did he agree with *Hippocrates,* but he actually confessed, blushing the way spirits blush, that he had always suspected it was so.

Pericles, who had approached the window, heaved a great sigh, of which I guessed the cause. He was reading an issue of *Le Moniteur,* which announced the decline of the arts and sciences; he saw illustrious scholars abandoning their sublime speculations to invent new crimes, and shuddered to hear a horde of cannibals compare themselves to the heroes of valiant Greece as without shame or remorse they sent venerable old men and women and children to their death on the scaffold, committing, in cold blood, the most atrocious and useless crimes.

Plato, who had listened to our conversation without saying a word, seeing it come to an unexpected end, began himself to speak.—''I can understand,'' he said, ''how the discoveries that your great men have made in all branches of the natural sciences would be useful to medicine, which will never alter the course of nature except at the cost of human life. Yet the same, no doubt, should not hold true for the research that has been done in the field of politics. *Locke*'s inquiries into the nature of human understanding, the invention of the printing press, the accumulation of understanding drawn from history, all the profound books that have spread science

78

even to the common people—all these wonders, in short, must surely have helped to make men better, have they not? —And the happy, wise republic I had imagined, which the age in which I lived considered an impracticable dream—surely this exists in the world today?'' In response to these questions, the good doctor could but cast his eyes down and shed a few tears; and as he was wiping them with his handkerchief, he inadvertently turned his wig in such a way that it covered part of his face. "Immortal gods!" said *Aspasia,* giving a shrill cry, "what an odd face! Was it also one of your great men's discoveries that led you to conceive of dressing your head with another man's skull?"

Aspasia, in whom the disquisitions of philosophers inspired only the desire to yawn, had laid her hands upon a fashion journal lying on the mantelpiece and had been flipping through it for some time when the doctor's wig elicited that exclamation from her; and as the narrow, unsteady chair in which she sat was rather uncomfortable to her, she had, without ceremony, placed her bare legs, adorned with thongs, upon the straw chair that stood between her and me, leaning her elbow on one of *Plato*'s broad shoulders.

"It's not a skull," replied the doctor, taking his wig in hand and tossing it into the fire, "it's a wig, Mademoiselle, and I know not why I did not throw this ridiculous ornament into the flames of Tartarus when I first arrived among you. But ridiculous customs and prejudices are so deeply ingrained in our petty nature that they follow us for a while even beyond the grave.''—I was singularly amused to see doctor abjure at once his medicine and his wig.

"I can assure you," said *Aspasia* to him, "that most of the hairstyles presented in this booklet I have been leafing through deserve the same fate as yours."—The beautiful Athenian was enjoying herself immensely as she perused those prints, and she had every reason to wonder at the variety and extravagance of modern adornments. One figure especially caught her eye, that of a young lady presented in a coiffure of the most elegant sort, which *Aspasia* found a bit too high; on the other hand, the veil covering her bust was so vast that scarcely half her face was visible. Not knowing that these extraordinary shapes were but the product of starch, *Aspasia* could not help but express amazement, though her surprise would have been doubly great, for the opposite reason, had the veil been transparent.

"But tell us," she said, "why do today's women seem to wear clothes to hide themselves rather than to dress themselves? They hardly even show their faces, though that is the sole means whereby one might tell their sex, so misshapen are their figures by the bizarre pleats of the fabrics they wear. Of all the fashions presented in these pages, not one leaves the throat, arms, or legs uncovered: why have your young warriors not attempted to destroy such a custom? Apparently," she added, "the virtue of today's women, which can be seen in all their clothing, is far greater than that of my contemporaries."—In finishing this statement, *Aspasia* looked at me as if expecting a reply.—I pretended not to notice;—and to give the appearance of distraction, I took the tongs and pushed the remainder of the doctor's wig, which had escaped the fire, onto the hot embers.—Then I noticed, however, that one of the thongs fastening *Aspasia*'s buskin had come untied. "My lovely lady," I said, "please allow me"—and so saying, I bent down briskly, bringing my hands to the chair where I truly believed I was seeing the legs that long ago had made great philosophers rave.

I am convinced that, at that moment, I was in a state of true somnambulism, for the movement I just mentioned was quite real; *Rosine*, however, who lay in fact on that chair, assumed the gesture to be for her and, hopping lightly into my arms, dispatched the famous shades evoked by my traveling coat back to the underworld.

Imagination, realm of enchantment!—which the most beneficent of beings bestowed upon man to console him for reality—I must quit you now. Today is the day that certain people, upon whom my fate depends, presume to give me back my freedom—as if they had taken it away from me! As if it were in their power to steal it from me and prevent me from traveling, as I please, the vast, ever open space before me!—They may have forbidden me to travel through a city, one place, but they left me the entire universe: infinity and eternity are at my command.

So today is the day of my freedom, or rather the day that I shall put my shackles back on. The yoke of worldly matters will weigh heavy on me once again; I shall no longer take a single step that is not measured by decorum and duty.—And I shall be happy simply if some capricious goddess does not make me forget both! And if I can escape this new and dangerous captivity!

Why did they not let me finish my voyage! Was it thus to punish me that they confined me to my room?—To that enchanted realm containing all the wealth and riches of the world? One might as well exile a mouse to a granary.

Meanwhile, never have I been more keenly aware of my *double* nature.—Even as I regret the loss of my imaginary pleasures, I feel consoled in spite of myself: a mysterious force compels me—it tells me I am in need of air and sky, and that solitude resembles death.—So here I am now, all decked out;—my front door opens;—I wander under the spacious arcades of the rue du Pô; a thousand amiable ghosts hover before my eyes;—yes, that's the building, all right—the door, the staircase;—I shudder in anticipation.

Similarly, one has a sour foretaste on the tongue when cutting a lemon before eating it.

Poor *animal!* Be on your guard!

NOCTURNAL EXPEDITION
AROUND MY ROOM
(1825)

CHAPTER I

To spark some interest in the new room in which I have just conducted a nocturnal expedition, I ought to explain how this dwelling fell to my lot. Forever distracted from my occupations by the noise in the house where I used to live, I had long intended to find myself a more solitary retreat in the neighborhood; then one day, while reading a biographical note on de Buffon,* I learned that this famous man had chosen to work in a secluded cottage in his gardens, with no furniture but an armchair and the desk on which he wrote, and no work of literature but the manuscript on which he was working at the time.

Yet the chimerae which engage my attentions are so vastly incomparable to the immortal works of de Buffon that the idea of imitating him, even in that respect, would probably never have crossed my mind if not for two mishaps that occurred in rapid succession. When dusting the furniture one day, a servant, believing he saw a great deal of dust on a pastel that I had just finished, wiped it so thoroughly with his cloth that he managed to rid it of all the dust that I had so carefully put there.

I had scarcely recovered from this unfortunate oc-
curence when another, even crueler than the first,
succeeded in exhausting my patience. A young niece
of mine got it into her head to lick a portrait in
miniature, and when she noticed that the colors thus
became brighter, she repeated the action, and in the
process the moistened paint passed entirely onto her
tongue.

After having scolded and kissed the little girl, I
went into action straightaway and returned home
with the key to a small fifth-floor room I had rented
in the rue *de la Providence*.* I had all the materials
of my favorite pursuits brought there the same day,
and thereafter spent the greater part of my time shel-
tered from the din of the home and its picture-
cleaners.

The hours flew by like minutes in my solitary
garret, and more than once my daydreams made me
forget that it was dinner time.

O sweet solitude! I have known the charms with
which you intoxicate your admirers. Woe to the man
who cannot be alone for a single hour of his life
without feeling the torment of ennui, and who would
rather, if he must, converse with fools than with
himself!

Yet I must confess that I love solitude in big cities.
And unless constrained by some grave occasion such
as a voyage around my room, I want to be a hermit
only in the morning; evenings, I like to see human
faces again, for there are some that are so lovely!
The drawbacks of social life and those of solitude

thus nullify one another, while each mode of existence enhances the other.

The things of this world are so fickle and doomed to misfortune that the very intensity of the pleasures I enjoyed in my new dwelling ought to have forewarned me as to how very briefly they would last. The French Revolution, which was spilling over on all sides, had just crossed the Alps and was descending on Italy. The first wave swept me all the way to Bologna. I kept my hermitage, into which I had moved all my furniture, until happier days should come. Having already been for several years without a country, one fine morning I learned I was also out of work. After spending a whole year seeing people and things scarcely to my liking, and wishing for things and people I no longer saw, I went back to Turin.* I had to make a decision. I left the Hotel *de la Bonne Femme,* where I had taken up, with a view to giving the little room back to the landlord and getting rid of my furniture.

It is difficult to describe the feelings that came over me as I entered my hermitage again. Everything was in the same order, that is, the same disorder in which I had left it: the furniture stacked against the walls had been protected from dust by the altitude of the apartment; my quills were still in the dried-up inkstand, and on the table I found an unfinished letter.

I still feel at home here, I said to myself with genuine satisfaction. Each object recalled some event of my life; my room was a tapestry of memories. Instead of returning to the hotel, I decided to spend the night in the company of my possessions. I sent for my valise, and at the same time resolved to depart the following day, without notifying or consulting anyone, entrusting my fate entirely to Providence.

CHAPTER II

While I was absorbed in these thoughts, fairly congratulating myself for conceiving such an excellent travel plan, the time flew by and my manservant had not returned. He was a man whom necessity had compelled me to take into my service several weeks before and whose trustworthiness I had begun to doubt. When all at once it occurred to me that he might have made off with my suitcase, I raced to the hotel: I was just in time. As I was turning the corner of the street of the Hotel *de la Bonne Femme,* I saw him dash hurriedly out the door behind a porter carrying my valise. He had taken charge of my money box himself; and instead of turning in my direction, he headed left, away from where he should have been going. His intention was clear. I easily caught up with him and, saying nothing, walked beside him a while before he took any notice. If one had wished to portray the expression of astonishment and fright taken to its highest degree in the human countenance, he would have been the perfect model, at the moment when he spotted me beside him. I had all the time I needed to study him, for he was so flabbergasted by my sudden appearance and the gravity with which I looked at him, that he kept walking a spell beside me, as if we were out on a stroll together. At last he mumbled an excuse about some business he had in rue *Grand-Doire;* I put him back on the right road, however, and when we returned to my apartment, I dismissed him.

Only then did I resolve to embark on a new voyage around my room, on the last night I was to spend there, and I began to make preparations at once.

CHAPTER III

For a long time I had yearned to return to the country I was so delighted to visit long ago; moreover, my description of it seemed incomplete to me. A few friends who had shared in its pleasures begged me to continue it, and I should, no doubt, have made up my mind to do so sooner, had I not been separated from my traveling companions. I resumed my course with reluctance. I was, alas! setting off alone. I would be traveling without my cherished Joanetti and without my sweet Rosine. My first room had itself undergone the most disastrous of revolutions— what am I saying?—it no longer existed: its outer wall, which at the time formed part of a dreadful warren, was blackened by the flames, and every murderous contrivance of war had combined to destroy it utterly.* A cannonball had pierced the wall on which the portrait of Mme de Hautcastel was hung. In short, had I not been so lucky as to undertake my voyage before this catastrophe, today's scholars would never have come to know that remarkable room. Similarly, without the observations of Hipparchus, they would not know today that the Pleiad had once contained another star, which has disappeared since the time of that famous astronomer.*

Compelled by circumstances, I had already quit my room some time before and taken my penates elsewhere. That's not such a tragedy, you will say. Yet how shall I ever replace Joanetti and Rosine? It's not possible, alas. Joanetti had become so indispensable to me that I shall never make up for his loss. Who, moreover, can claim to live forever with the people he cherishes? Like those swarms of gnats that one sees swirling in the air on fine summer evenings, people come together purely by chance and only very briefly—and they are lucky if, in their rapid movements, they are as adroit as the gnats and do not break their heads running into each other!

One evening I was getting into bed. Joanetti was attending to me with his customary zeal, and actually seemed more solicitous than usual. As he took the lamp away, I turned my eyes to him and noticed a distinct change in his features. Was I to conclude from this that poor Joanetti was serving me for the last time?—But I do not wish to keep the reader in a state of suspense crueler than the truth itself. I would rather tell him straightaway that Joanetti got married that same night and left me the following day.

Let no one, however, accuse him of ingratitude for having quit his master so abruptly. I had long known of his intention, and had been wrong to oppose it. A busybody came to me early that morning to bring me the news, and this gave me time to lose my temper and calm back down before seeing Joanetti again, thus sparing him the reproaches he expected. Before entering my room, in fact, he made a show of speaking loudly to someone from the gallery, to make me think he wasn't afraid; then arming himself with as much impudence as a soul so good as his could muster, he presented himself with a look of determination. On his face I immediately read everything that was happening in his soul and held none of it against him. In this day and age, cynics have so frightened honest folk as to the dangers of marriage that a newly married man often looks like someone who has just had a terrifying fall without coming to any harm and is simultaneously overwhelmed with fear and satisfaction, which makes him look ridiculous. It was therefore not surprising that my faithful servant's behavior should betray the peculiarity of his situation.

"So you're married now, are you, my dear Joanetti?" I said to him laughing. As he had prepared himself only against an outburst of anger on my part, all his precautions were for naught. He immediately fell back into his customary disposition, and even a bit lower, for he began to weep.

"What can I say, Monsieur?" he said in a strained voice, "I had given my word."

"Well, by God, you did the right thing, old friend. May you be happy as can be with your wife, and especially with yourself! May you be blessed with children just like you! So now we shall have to part ways!"

"Yes, Monsieur. We plan to settle in Asti."

"And when do you wish to leave me?"

Here Joanetti lowered his eyes bashfully, and replied in a much softer tone: "My wife has found a coachman from her town, who is returning with an empty coach; he is leaving today. It would be an excellent opportunity . . .; but I will go, of course, when it pleases Monsieur . . . although a similar opportunity is unlikely to arise again."

"What! so soon?" I said. A sense of fondness and regret, mingled with a strong dose of displeasure, held my tongue momentarily. "But no," I replied rather harshly, "of course I'll not detain you; leave right now, if that suits your convenience." Joanetti turned pale. "Go on, old friend, go to your wife; and be always as decent and honorable with her as you have been with me." After we had settled a few matters, I sadly bade him farewell, and he left.

That man had served me for fifteen years. We were separated in an instant. I have not seen him since.

Pacing about my room, I pondered this sudden separation. Rosine had followed Joanetti without his noticing. Fifteen minutes later, the door opened and Rosine came inside. I could see Joanetti's hand push her into the room; as the door closed again, I felt my heart sink. Already he refrains from setting foot in my house! A few minutes had sufficed to make strangers of two companions of fifteen years. O sad, sad human fate, never to have a single lasting object in which to place the least of one's affections!

CHAPTER IV

Rosine, too, lived far from me then. You will, no doubt, be interested to learn, my dear Marie,* that at fifteen years of age she was still the most lovable of creatures, and that the same superior intelligence that formerly set her apart from the rest of her species also helped her to bear the weight of old age. I should have preferred never to part company with her; yet when the fate of our friends is at stake, should we not look only to their interest and their pleasure? It was in Rosine's interest to quit the itinerant life she led with me and to savor at last, in her latter days, a tranquillity that her master could no longer hope for. A charitable nun agreed to take care of her for the rest of her days; and I know that in this retirement she enjoyed all the advantages that her merits, her age, and her reputation had so rightfully earned her.

And since the nature of man is such that happiness seems not his destiny; since friend offends friend without meaning to, and even lovers cannot live without quarreling; in short, since from the time of Lycurgus to this very day all legislators have failed in their attempts to make men happy, my consolation will be, at least, to have made a dog happy.

CHAPTER V

Now that I have given the reader the last details of the story of Joanetti and Rosine, I need only say a word about the soul and the beast to fulfill all my obligations to him. These two characters, especially the latter, will no longer play so important a role in my voyage. An amiable traveler who followed the same path as I* claims that they must be weary by now. He is, alas, only too right. Not that my soul has grown any less active, as least as far as she can tell; rather, her relations with the *other* have changed. The latter is not, perhaps, as sharp in his repartee as he once was; he no longer has—how shall I put it? I was about to say he no longer has the same presence of mind, as if a beast could have any such thing! In any event, to avoid cumbersome explanations, I shall say only that, lately spurred by the apparent encouragements of a certain Alexandrine, I wrote this young lady a rather affectionate letter, only to receive a polite but cold reply that concluded with the elegant words: "Please rest assured, Monsieur, that the sincere esteem I feel for you will ever remain." Good heavens! I cried out, I am finished. Since that fateful day, I have resolved to cease expounding my system of the soul and the beast. Accordingly, no longer distinguishing between the two beings and no longer separating them, I shall pass them off as one package, the one including the other, as certain merchants do with their wares, and I shall travel henceforth as a single unit, to avoid all inconveniences.

Chapter VI

It would be pointless to discuss the dimensions of my new room. It is so similar to the first one that upon first glance one might mistake it for that room, if the architect had not taken care to make the ceiling slant obliquely toward the street, leaving the roof to slope in the direction required by the laws of hydraulics for draining the rainwater. The daylight enters through a single window two-and-one-half feet wide and four feet tall, situated at a height of six to seven feet from the floor, and accessible by a small ladder.

The placement of the window so high above the

floor is one of those fortunate occurrences that might as likely be due to chance as to the genius of the architect. The nearly perpendicular light that it used to diffuse in my garret created an atmosphere of mystery. The ancient temple of the Pantheon in Rome receives the light in more or less the same manner. In addition, there was nothing outside that might distract me. Like those navigators lost over the vast ocean sea, who see nothing but sky and water, I saw only sky and my room, and the nearest external things on which my gaze might alight were the moon and the morning star. This put me in direct contact with the heavens and enabled my thoughts to soar to a loftier height than they could ever have done had I taken a lodging on the ground floor.

The window in question jutted out above the roof and formed a very pretty dormer: so high above the horizon was it, in fact, that whenever the sun's first rays began to brighten it, the streets were still dark. The view I enjoyed was also one of the loveliest imaginable. Yet even the most beautiful view becomes tiresome if one sees it too often: the eye grows accustomed to it and soon one no longer takes any note of it. The placement of my window spared me this unpleasantness as well, for I could never see the wondrous sight of the Turinese countryside without climbing four or five steps, which always gave me a tremendous thrill, since I enjoyed it sparingly. Whenever, weary from travel and the profound meditations that this required of me, I wished to afford myself some delightful amusement, I would end my day by climbing up to my window.

At the first step of the ladder, I would still see nothing but sky; but soon the enormous temple of the Superga would begin to come into view.* The hill of Turin, on which it stands, would slowly rise up before me, covered with forests and sumptuous vineyards, proudly offering up its gardens and palaces to the setting sun while the simpler, modest abodes seemed half-hidden in its dales, the better to serve as refuge to the wise man and favor his contemplations.

Charming hill, you have often seen me seek out your solitary recesses, preferring your untraveled paths to the bright boulevards of the capital; you have often seen me lost in your labyrinths of green, listening for the lark's song in morning, my heart filled with a vague unrest and the burning desire to settle down forever in your enchanted vales.—I salute you, charming hill! Your image is forever etched in my memory. May the heavenly dew, if such is possible, make your fields more fertile and your groves more verdant! May your inhabitants savor their happiness in peace, may the shade of your branches favor them with health and contentment! And may your happy land forever remain the sweet refuge of the true philosophy, humble knowledge, and sincere and generous friendship I have found there.

CHAPTER VII

I began my journey at exactly eight o'clock in the evening. The weather was fair; it promised to be a lovely night. I had taken measures so as not to be diverted from my course by any visits—which are very infrequent at the altitude at which I lived, especially in such circumstances as mine at that moment—and to be left alone until midnight. Four hours would suffice to carry out my undertaking, for this time I intended only to take a brief nocturnal tour around my room. If my first voyage had lasted forty-two days, it was because it was not within my power to shorten it. Nor did I wish to subject myself to traveling by coach as before, for I was convinced that a traveler on foot sees a great many things that elude one who is moving posthaste. I therefore decided to travel alternately, and as circumstance might dictate, on foot and on horseback—a new method I have yet to explain, the usefulness of which will soon become clear. Lastly, I intended to take notes along the way, and to write down my observations as I made them, so as not to forget anything.

To give some order to my undertaking, and to allow it a chance to succeed as before, I decided I should begin by composing a dedicatory epistle, and that I should write it in verse to make it more interesting. Two problems hindered me, however, and nearly made me give up the idea, despite the great advantage I might gain from it. The first was that of knowing to whom I should address the epistle; the second, how I should go about writing verse. After having pondered the matter closely, I was quick to realize that it made sense first to write my epistle as best I could, and then to find somebody to whom it might be appropriate to address it. I set to work at once, and labored for more than an hour without managing to find a rhyme to the first line I had written, which had seemed to me a very good line. I then remembered, in rather timely fashion, that the great Alexander Pope never composed anything of worth without first forcing himself to declaim loudly and at length, and moving all about his study, to whet his spirit. I attempted at once to imitate him. I took a volume of Ossian's poems and recited them at the top of my voice, pacing in great strides to work myself up to a state of inspiration.

I soon noticed, however, that the difficulty of pronouncing the bizarre names of the characters in the poem was dampening my imagination instead of exciting it. When, in reading, I came upon the names Bobarduthul or Mackormac, I stopped short and was forced to begin again. I did not give up, however, and to loosen my tongue, since, unlike Demosthenes, I did not have any pebbles at hand,* I wrote down on a piece of paper, in succession, all the poetic, sonorous names used by that famous Scotsman and began to walk around the room, pronouncing each distinctly, one after another, as rapidly and loudly as possible.

MACKORMAC, CUCHULLIN, CHROTAR, BOR-
BARDUTHUL, CONNACHAR, CONNAL.

As I pronounced each word, a slight shudder
coursed through my entire body, as when hearing an
iron rod being sawed. At first I took this new sensation for an initial spark of inspiration, and I continued my recitation with redoubled passion, raising
my voice an octave higher.

COLCULLA, COLDERHA, COHLAMA, CONMOR,
CROMAR, CROMAGLAS, CULALIN, CURAC.

I leaned for a moment against the wall, to catch
my breath.

FOVARGORMO, KINFEHA, OICHOMA, CU-
THONA, TROMATON, TURLATHON, TURLOG.

At last no longer able to control myself, and determined to compose an epistle in verse at all costs, I
began to leap and flail about my room in such a
frenzy that I should certainly have produced a masterpiece*, had I not forgotten about the slope in the
ceiling, the steep decline of which prevented my
forehead from proceeding as far forward as my feet
in the direction I had taken—I banged my head so
hard against that blasted barrier that it shook the
building's roof: the sparrows sleeping under the tiles
all took flight in terror, and I myself rebounded three
steps back.

As I was struggling thus to whet my spirit, a pretty young woman from the floor below, alarmed by the racket I was making, and thinking perhaps I was giving a dance in my room, delegated her husband to find the cause of the noise. I was still dazed from the contusion I had sustained when the door opened slightly. An elderly man, with melancholy mien, poked his head forward and glanced curiously about the room. When he had overcome his surprise at finding me alone, he said in an angry tone: "My wife has a migraine, Monsieur. I will have you know—" But I interrupted him at once, and my style reflected the loftiness of my thoughts at that moment.

"—Worthy messenger of the fair Kinfeha," I said to him in the language of the bards, "why do thine eyes shine 'neath thy bushy brows like two meteors in the black forest of Cromba? Thy lovely mate is a ray of light, and I would fain die a thousand deaths ere I troubled her repose; yet thy mien, O worthy messenger, thy mien is like the remotest vault of the cavern of Carmora when storm clouds gather to blacken night's face and weigh heavy o'er the silent wolds of Morven."

The neighbor, who apparently had never read the poems of Ossian, regrettably mistook my surge of inspiration for a fit of madness and seemed quite perplexed. As I had no intention whatsoever of offending him, I offered him a chair and said to him in the most affable tone:

FOVARGORMO, KINFEHA, OICHOMA, CUTHON, TROMATHOH, TURLATON, TURLOK.

I might well have said more, but I noticed he was quietly withdrawing. He was making the sign of the cross, saying under his breath: *"E' matto, per Bacco, è matto!"**

CHAPTER IX

I sat down at my desk to record these events, as I always do; but no sooner did I open a drawer with the intention of finding some paper in it, than I closed it again abruptly, troubled by one of the most unpleasant feelings that one can have, that of humbled pride. The manner of surprise by which I was caught on this occasion was much like that which a thirsty traveler experiences when, bringing his lips to the limpid pool, he espies a frog staring up at him from the bottom. What I had seen, however, was only the springs and carcass of an artificial dove which, following Archytas's example, I had once endeavored to make fly through the air.* I had labored without respite at its construction for more than three months. On the day of the great test, I placed it at the edge of a table, having carefully closed the door, to keep the invention a secret and give my friends a pleasant surprise. The mechanism was held down by a string. Who can even imagine how my heart fluttered, how my pride trembled in anguish as I brought the scissors near to sever that fateful bond? Then, presto! . . . the dove's spring is released and uncoils noisily. I look up to see it fly past; but after making a few turns by itself, it falls and runs under the table. Rosine, who was sleeping there, walked glumly away. Rosine, who never saw a chicken, pigeon, or even the tiniest bird without attacking and chasing it, did not even deign to glance at my dove as it floundered across the floor. . . . It was a fatal blow to my pride. I went out on the ramparts for a breath of air.

CHAPTER X

Such was the fate of my artificial dove. While my mechanical genius had destined it to follow the eagle in the heavens, fate had given it the instincts of a mole.

I was walking alone, sad and discouraged, as one always is after great hopes are dashed, when I looked up and saw a flock of cranes flying over my head. I stopped to contemplate them. They were advancing in triangular formation, like the English column at the battle of Fontenoy. I watched them cross the sky from cloud to cloud. "Ah, how well they fly!" I said to myself under my breath, "how confidently they seem to glide along the invisible path they follow!"—Shall I say it? May I be forgiven, alas! Once, and only once, has the horrible feeling of envy entered my heart, and it was for those cranes. My jealous eyes pursued them to the limits of the horizon. I stood a long time amidst the passing crowd, motionless, studying the swift movements of the swallows, astonished to see them suspended in air, as if I had never before witnessed such a phenomenon. A sense of profound admiration, hitherto unknown to me, brightened my spirit. I thought I was seeing nature for the first time. I listened in surprise to the buzzing of flies, the twitter of birds, and that mysterious, confused sound of living creation involuntarily celebrating its creator. An ineffable chorus, which man alone has the sublime privilege of being able to supplement with a note of gratitude! "Who conceived this brilliant mechanism?" I cried out in my rapture. "Who is it that, opening his life-giving hand, set the first swallow free on the wind?—Who ordered the trees to sprout up from the earth and raise their branches to the heavens?—And you, ravishing creature, who move so majestically in their shade, you whose countenance commands respect and love, who put you on the surface of the earth to embellish it thus? What mind conceived the plan of those forms divine, with a power so great it could create the gaze and smile of innocent beauty? . . . And I myself, who feel my own heart flutter . . . what is the purpose of my existence?—What am I, where do I come from, I the creator of the centripetal artificial dove?! . . ."

Scarcely had I uttered those brutal words when, suddenly regaining my senses like a sleeping man on whom one has thrown a bucket of water, I realized that a number of people had gathered round to examine me as I spoke to myself in my transport. I then espied the lovely Georgine a few steps ahead of me. The portion of her left cheek, covered with rouge, that I glimpsed through the curls of her blond wig succeeded in bringing me back in touch with the things of this world, from which I had momentarily absented myself.

CHAPTER XI

Once I had recovered somewhat from the distraction occasioned me by the sight of my artificial dove, the pain of the bump I had received began to make itself keenly felt. I ran my hand over my forehead and noticed a new protuberance in exactly the same part of the head where Dr. Gall had situated the poetic protuberance.* At the time, however, I had given it no thought; experience alone was to prove to me the truth of that famous man's system.

After collecting myself for a moment before making one final stab at my dedicatory epistle, I seized a pen and set to work. To my great surprise, the lines flowed of themselves from my hand! I filled two pages in less than an hour, and concluded from this fact that if it was necessary for Pope to move his head to compose verse, mine required nothing less than a contusion. I will not, however, show the reader what I wrote, for the prodigious speed with which the adventures of my journey followed one upon another prevented me from putting the finishing touches on it. This reticence notwithstanding, there can be no doubt that my accident ought to be considered a most valuable discovery, one which poets could never use too much.*

Indeed, so convinced am I of the infallibility of this new method, that in a poem of twenty-four cantos that I have since composed, which will be published with *La Prisonnière de Pignerol,* I have found it thus far unnecessary to pen any lines of verse; I have, however, made a fair copy of five hundred pages of notes—which, as we know, always form the most interesting, and voluminous, part of the majority of modern poems.

Walking aimlessly about my room as I deeply pondered my discoveries, I then stumbled over my bed and fell upon it in a sitting position; as my hand had perchance come down upon my nightcap, I decided to cover my head with it and go to bed.

Chapter XII

I had been in bed a quarter of an hour, and most unusual for me, I was not yet asleep. The thought of my dedicatory epistle had been followed by the saddest of reflections: my candle, which was nearing its end, no longer cast but an uneven, gloomy light from the bottom of the sconce, and my room seemed like a tomb.

A sudden gust of wind opened the window, blew out my light, and slammed the door shut. My somber cast of mind grew even blacker with the darkness.

All my past pleasures and all my present woes bore down at once upon my heart and filled it with regret and bitterness.

Though I make a constant effort to forget my troubles and banish them from my thoughts, sometimes, when I am not careful, they flood my memory all at once, as if a sluice gate had been opened. On such occasions I have no choice but to abandon myself to the torrent bearing me away, and then my thoughts become so black, every object begins to look so sinister to me, that I usually end up laughing at my folly—and thus the cure is found in the violence of the ailment itself.

I was still in the throes of one of these bouts of melancholy when part of the blast of wind that had opened my window and shut my door in passing after blowing round the room several times, leafing through my books, and throwing a loose sheet of my journey onto the floor, at last penetrated my bed curtains and came to die on my cheek. I felt the night's gentle chill and, considering this an invitation on its part, I got up at once and climbed my ladder to enjoy the tranquillity of nature.

CHAPTER XIII

It was a clear night. The Milky Way divided the sky like a wisp of cloud; each star cast a gentle beam that traveled all the way to me, and when I looked at one more carefully than the rest, its companions seemed to twinkle more brightly to catch my eye.

The charm of contemplating the starry sky is one that never fades for me, and I can say, to my satisfaction, that I have never taken a single voyage, or even a simple stroll, without paying my tribute of admiration to the wonders of the firmament. Though in such lofty meditations I may sense the powerlessness of my own thought, I find pleasures beyond words in them. I like to think that it is not chance that brings these emanations of distant worlds to my eyes, while with its light each star pours a ray of hope into my heart.—What's that? Might these wonders have no other connection to me than their twinkling in my eyes? Is it possible they have no idea that my thoughts soar to their height, or that my heart flutters at the sight of them? . . . The ephemeral spectator of an eternal spectacle, man raises his eyes a moment to the sky, then shuts them forever; yet during that brief moment granted him, from every point of the sky, from every limit of the universe, a consoling beam is cast from each world and meets his gaze to tell him that there is indeed a connection between infinity and him, and that he is part of eternity.

CHAPTER XIV

An annoying thought, however, disturbed the pleasure I took in giving myself over to these reflections. How few people—I said to myself—are sharing my enjoyment of this sublime spectacle, which the heavens waste on the sleeping multitudes. . . . But never mind those who are asleep: what would it cost those who are out for a walk, those emerging en masse from the theatre, to look up a moment and admire the glittering constellations shining everywhere over their heads?—No, the rapt audience of Jocrisse or Scapin will not deign to raise their eyes:* they will go home or elsewhere like brutes, never thinking that the sky exists. The fools! . . . Merely because one can see it often and free of charge, they want no part of it. Now if the firmament were always concealed from us, if the spectacle it offers us were dependent upon some impresario, the first-row boxes on the roofs would price out of the market, and the ladies of Turin would seize my dormer window.

"Oh, if only I were ruler of some land," I exclaimed, overcome with righteous indignation, "I should sound the tocsin every night, and make all my subjects, of every age, sex, and social station, stand at their windows and gaze at the stars." But here reason, whose right of remonstrance in my kingdom is contested at best, was more successful than usual in the objections she made to the ill-considered edict I wished to promulgate in my realm. "Sire," she said to me, "would your majesty not deign perhaps to make an exception for rainy nights since, in such cases, the sky being overcast—" "—Very well, very well," I replied, "I hadn't thought of that: let it be noted, then, that rainy nights are excepted." "—Sire," she continued, "I think it might also be advisable to make exceptions for clear nights when it is too cold and north wind is blowing, since strict observance of the edict would overwhelm your happy subjects with colds and coughs." I was beginning to see many problems in the execution of my plan, and yet it pained me to give it up. "We must write," said I, "to the Council of Medicine and to the Academy of Science to determine the degree on the centigrade thermometer at which my subjects can be excused from standing at their windows: but I want, I absolutely insist, that that my order be carried out to the letter." "—What about the infirm, Sire?" "—That goes without saying; they shall be exempt: humaneness must come first." "—If I did not fear importuning your majesty, I should also point out to him that one could (in the event that he deemed it appropriate and found no great inconvenience in it) also make an exception for the blind, since, being deprived of the power of sight—" "—Well, is that all?" I interrupted testily." "—I do beg your pardon, Sire, but what about loving couples? Surely your majesty's gentle heart could not force them to look at the stars too?" "—All right, all right; let us defer the matter for now; we shall have to think it over. You shall present me a detailed memorandum on it."

God almighty! How many considerations must be made before issuing an important police ordinance!

Chapter xv

The brightest stars have never been the ones I gaze upon with greatest pleasure; rather, it is the smallest stars, the ones that, lost in an immeasurable remoteness, seem but imperceptible points in the sky, which have always been my favorites. The reason for this is quite simple: one will easily understand that by letting my imagination travel as far beyond their sphere as my gaze does on this side just to reach them, I find myself effortlessly transported a distance that few travelers before me have reache once there, I am astonished to find that I am still only at the beginning of this vast universe: for it would, I believe, be ridiculous to think that there exists a barrier beyond which nothingness begins, as if nothingness were easier to understand than existence! Beyond the last star, I can imagine yet another, which would not be the last one either. By assigning limits to creation, however distant, the universe becomes for me a mere point of light in comparison with the immensity of empty space surrounding it, the dark, horrible nothingness in the middle of which it would presumably be suspended like a solitary lamp.—Here I covered my eyes with my hands, to banish all manner of distraction and to afford my thoughts the profundity required by such a subject; and, making a supernatural effort of mind, I composed a system of the universe, the most complete that has yet been conceived. Here it is, in all its details; it is the result of all my life's reflections: "I believe that since space . . ."—But it merits a chapter of its own; and given the importance of the subject, it will be the only chapter of my journey with a title.

Chapter XVI

The System of the Universe

I believe, then, that since space is infinite, creation must be as well, and that God in his eternity created an infinity of worlds in the vastness of space.

Chapter XVII

I will admit in all good faith that I understand my system not a whit, no more than I do all the other systems thus far hatched from the imaginations of philosophers past and present. Mine, however, has the precious advantage of being contained in three lines, despite its immensity. The indulgent reader will also note that it was composed, in its entirety, atop a ladder. All the same, I should have embellished it with commentaries and notes if, at the moment I was most deeply engrossed in my subject, I had not been distracted by some enchanting sounds that sweetly fell upon my ear. Not far from me a voice more melodious than any I had ever heard, even that of Zénéide, one of those voices that are forever attuned to my heartstrings, was singing a love song of which I missed not a word, and which I shall never forget. As I listened with rapt attention, I discovered that the voice was coming from a window lower than mine, which unfortunately I could not see; the eaves of the roof from which my dormer window rose up concealed it from my view.

Meanwhile the desire to catch a glimpse of the siren charming me with her refrains increased in proportion to the charm of her ballad, whose touching words would have moved even the most callous lout to tears. Soon, no longer able to resist my curiosity, I climbed up to the last step of the ladder, placed one foot on the edge of the roof and, holding onto the cheek of the dormer with one hand, I suspended myself over the void, at the risk of falling into the street.

At once I noticed on the balcony to my left, just below me, a young woman in a white dressing gown; she was resting her lovely head in her hand, inclining it just enough to afford a glimpse, with the aid of the starlight, of a most interesting profile, and her posture seemed intended to present in its finest light, to an airborne traveler such as I, a slender, shapely figure; one of her bare feet, thrust casually behind her, was turned in such a manner that I could easily imagine, in spite of the dark, its exquisite shape, while a pretty little slipper, from which it was separated, defined it even better for my inquisitive eyes. You can well imagine, my dear Sophie,* the frantic state I was in. I dared not make the slightest exclamation, for fear of startling my lovely neighbor, nor the slightest movement, for fear of plummeting into the street. A sigh escaped from me nonetheless, but I managed just in time to stifle half of it, while the rest was borne away by a passing zephyr. Now I had all the leisure I might want to contemplate the lovely stargazer, hanging in my perilous position by the hope of hearing her sing some more. But, alas! her song was over, and my cruel fate was keeping her most stubbornly silent. At last, having waited a rather long time, I felt I could venture to say a word to her: I needed only to think of a greeting equal to her and to the feelings she had inspired in me. O how I regretted not having finished my dedicatory epistle in verse! How useful it would have been on this occasion! My presence of mind did not, however, fail me in that moment of need. Inspired by the gentle influence of the stars and by the even stronger desire to make good with a beautiful woman, I lightly cleared my throat, to forewarn her and to soften the sound of my voice, and then I said in the tenderest tone possible: "What fine weather we are having tonight."

CHAPTER XVIII

I believe I can already hear Mme de Hautcastel, who never misses a thing, calling me to account for the love song I mentioned in the previous chapter. For the first time in my life, I am forced by dire necessity to refuse her something. If I inserted those verses in my voyage, people would inevitably take me for their author, which would give rise to more than a few bad jokes on the need for contusions, which I should like to avoid. I shall therefore continue the account of my adventure with my winsome neighbor, an adventure whose unforeseen conclusion, as well as the delicacy with which I carried it out, will not fail to interest every manner of reader. But, before learning what her reply to me was, and how my ingenious greeting was received, I must first respond to certain people who fancy themselves more eloquent than I and who will mercilessly condemn me for having begun the conversation in what may seem to them so trivial a manner. I shall prove to them that, if I had tried to be witty on that important occasion, I should have openly flouted the rules of discretion and good taste. Every man who begins a conversation with a beautiful woman with a witticism or a compliment, however flattering it may be, betrays expectations that ought not to be made manifest until they begin to have some basis in fact. If, moreover, he plays the wit, it is obvious he is trying to impress, and that therefore he is thinking more of himself than of his lady. Now ladies, of course, want us to devote our attentions to them, and though they may not think in exactly the same manner as I have just written, they nevertheless possess an exquisite, natural sense of taste whereby they know that a trivial statement, when uttered for the sole purpose of starting a conversation and approaching them, is a thousand times better than a stroke of wit inspired by vanity, and better still (which may come as some surprise) than a dedicatory epistle in verse. More than this, I maintain (even though my opinion may seem a paradox) that this light and sparkling spirit of conversation is not even necessary in a longer intimacy, if the bonds have been truly formed by the heart; and despite everything that people who have only loved with half a heart say about the long intervals that fall between the keen emotions of love and friendship, the day always passes more quickly when one spends it beside one's lady, and silence is just as interesting as discussion.

Whatever one may make of my argument, there is no doubt that I could find nothing better to say, on the edge of that roof, than the words in question. And no sooner did I utter them, than my entire soul rose to my eardrums to catch every last nuance of the sounds I hoped to hear. The beauty raised her head to look at me: her long hair unfurled like a sail and served as background to her lovely face as it reflected the mysterious light of the stars. Her lips were already parted, her sweet words pressing forward on her tongue. . . . But then—heavens above! To my great surprise and horror, a fatal sound was heard: "What are you doing there, Madame, at this hour of the night? Come back inside!" said a deep, male voice from within the apartment. I was petrified.

CHAPTER XIX

Such must be the sound that terrifies the sinners when the burning gates of Tartarus open suddenly before them—or better still, the sound made beneath the vaults of hell by the seven cataracts of the Styx, about which the poets have neglected to speak.

CHAPTER XX

A will-o'-the-wisp crossed the sky at that moment and disappeared almost at once. My eyes, which the meteor had drawn away for an instant, returned to the balcony to find only the little mule remaining there. In her hasty retreat, my pretty neighbor had forgotten to pick it up. I gazed a long time at that lovely mold of a foot worthy of Praxiteles' chisel, filled with an excitement the intensity of which I should never venture to confess; what may seem quite extraordinary, however—and I myself am at a loss to explain it—is that an irresistible attraction prevented me from taking my eyes off of it, try as I might to look at other things.

It is said that when a snake looks at a nightingale, the unlucky bird, victim of an irresistible spell, is compelled to approach the voracious reptile. Its swift wings no longer serve but to lead it to its destruction, and every effort it makes to escape only brings it closer to the enemy pursuing it with its unavoidable gaze.

Such was the effect that slipper had on me, though I cannot say with any certainty which of us, the slipper or I, was the snake, since according the laws of physics, the attraction must be the same in either case. Certainly its baneful influence was not a trick of my imagination: I was so truly, so strongly attracted that I was twice at the point of letting go with my hand and falling. However, as the balcony where I wanted to be was not directly under my window, but a little to one side, I saw quite clearly that when the force of gravity discovered by Newton was combined with the oblique attraction of the slipper, I should have fallen on a sentry box that from my height looked to me no larger than an egg, thus missing my target. . . . As a result I strengthened my grip on the window and, with a great effort of will, I managed to raise my eyes and look up at the sky.

CHAPTER XXI

I should be hard pressed to explain and define precisely the sort of pleasure I felt in this situation. All I can say with any assurance is that it had nothing in common with the delight I experienced a few moments earlier, at the sight of the Milky Way and the starry sky. All the same, as I have always liked to understand what is taking place in my soul at the most embarrassing moments of my life, so on this occasion I wanted to have a clear notion of the pleasure an honest man can experience when contemplating a lady's slipper, as compared to the pleasure to be had while contemplating the stars. With this end in view, I chose the sky with the most conspicuous constellation. It was, if I am not mistaken, Cassiopeia's Chair, which happened to be right above my head. I then looked by turns at the constellation and the slipper, and then at the slipper and the constellation, and I realized that these two sensations were each of a wholly different nature: one was in my head, while the other seemed to have its center in the region of my heart. Yet what I cannot confess without a touch of shame is that the charm that drew me to the enchanted slipper occupied all my other faculties as well. The rapture that the sight of the starry sky had inspired in me a short while earlier scarcely remained, and soon vanished altogether when I heard the balcony door open again and saw a satiny little foot, whiter than alabaster, come gently forward and take possession of the little mule. I wanted to say something; but, not having had the time to prepare myself as before, I no longer enjoyed my customary presence of mind, and I heard the balcony door close again before I could think of anything suitable to say.

CHAPTER XXII

The preceding chapters will, I hope, serve as a triumphant response to an accusation leveled by Mme de Hautcastel, who did not hesitate to denigrate my first voyage on the grounds that it afforded no occasion for making love. She cannot make the same criticism of this voyage; and although my adventure with my winsome neighbor was not carried very far, I can assure you that I derived more satisfaction from it than from many another circumstance in which I imagined I was happy because I had nothing with which to compare it. Everyone enjoys life in his own manner; but I believe I should fail in my duty to the reader's good will were I to keep him in the dark concerning a discovery which has contributed more than anything else to my happiness thus far—but let it be on the condition that it should remain between us: for I am speaking of nothing less than a new method of making love, far more advantageous than the previous one, with none of its countless inconveniences. As this discovery is especially intended for those who may wish to take up my new manner of travel, I believe I ought to devote a few chapters to their instruction.

CHAPTER XXIII

I had observed, over the course of my life, that
when I was in love according to the customary
method, my feelings were never equal to my hopes,
and my imagination was always thwarted in all its
designs. Pondering the matter carefully, I thought
that if I could extend the sentiment that quickens
me to individual love to include the entire sex that
is its object, I should enjoy unprecedented pleasures
without compromising myself in any way. How, indeed, could one reproach a man who happened to be
endowed with a heart energetic enough to love all the
lovable women in the world? Yes, Madame, I love
them all, not only those I know or hope to meet, but
all those living on the surface of the earth. More than
this, I love every woman who has ever lived, and
every one who will one day live, not to mention the
far greater number of those that my fancy conjures
up from nothingness. All possible women, in short,
are included in the vast circle of my affections.

What unjust, bizarre whim could ever possess me
to confine a heart like mine within the narrow limits
of a single community? Indeed, why circumscribe its
flight within the bounds of a kingdom or even a
republic?

Seated at the foot of an oak buffeted by the storm,
a young Indian widow mingles her sighs with the
howl of the unbridled winds. The arms of the warrior
she once loved hang over her head, and the mournful

sound they make as they clash recalls to her mind the memory of her past happiness. Meanwhile lightning bolts streak the clouds, their livid light reflecting in her motionless eyes. While the pyre that will consume her is being erected, she awaits, without solace, in the stupor of despair, the terrible death that a cruel prejudice makes her prefer to life.

What sweet and melancholy delight fills the heart of the sensitive man as he approaches that unlucky woman to console her! While I sit beside her on the grass, trying to dissuade her from that horrible sacrifice, mingling my sighs with hers and my tears with her tears, hoping to turn her thoughts away from her grief, the entire city is flocking to the home of Mme d'Antinal, whose husband has just died of a stroke. Also determined not to survive her husband, impervious to the tears and entreaties of her friends, she is letting herself die of hunger; and since this morning, when this news was imprudently brought to her, the poor woman has eaten but a biscuit and drunk but a little glass of Malaga wine. I give this disconsolate woman only the attention necessary to avoid transgressing the laws of my universal system, and then I quickly take my leave of her, for I am jealous by nature, and will not compromise myself with a crowd of comforters, nor with people too easily comforted.

Unhappy beauties have a special claim to my heart, and the sentitivity I am obliged to show them in no way diminishes my interest in happy beauties. This varies my pleasures infinitely, affording me the opportunity to go by turns from melancholy to good cheer, from sentimental tranquillity to the dance.

Often I form amorous liaisons in ancient history as well, obliterating whole entries in destiny's age-old registers. How many times have I not stayed the filicidal hand of Virginius and saved the life of his luckless daughter, victim of an excess of both crime and virtue! That event fills me with horror every time it comes back to me; I am not the least bit surprised that it started a revolution in the Roman empire.*

I hope that reasonable people, and compassionate souls, will be grateful to me for having settled this matter amicably. Any man who knows a little about the world will agree with me that, if one had let the decemvir have his way, that passionate man would not have failed to do justice to Virginia's honor: the parents would have intervened; papa Virginius, in the end, would have been appeased; and marriage would have followed, in accordance with all the forms required by law.

But what would have become of the poor abandoned lover? Well, what did the lover gain by the murder? But since you insist on feeling sorry for him, my dear Marie, let me inform you that six months after the death of Virginia, he not only got over that loss, but was quite happily married, and that after siring several children, he lost his wife as well and remarried six weeks after that, with the widow of a tribune of the plebs. These facts, hitherto unknown, were discovered and deciphered from a palimpsest of the Ambrosian Library by an Italian scholar of ancient history. They will, unfortunately, add yet another page to the abominable and already too long history of the Roman republic.

CHAPTER XXIV

After saving the lovely Virginia, I humbly avoid her effusions of gratitude and, ever desirous to be of service to beautiful women, I take advantage of the darkness of a rainy night to go open the tomb of a young vestal virgin whom the Roman Senate had the barbarism to bury alive for having let the sacred fire of Vesta go out, or perhaps for having lightly burned herself with it. I walk in silence through the winding streets of Rome, under that inner spell which precedes all good deeds, especially when there is some danger involved. I carefully avoid the Capitol, for fear of waking the geese, and slipping through the guards of the Colline Gate, I succeed in reaching the tomb unseen.

Upon hearing the sound I make lifting the stone that covers her, the unhappy girl raises her disheveled head from the damp floor of the burial vault. By the light of the sepulchral lamp, I see her looking wildly about her: in her delirium, the wretched victim thinks she is already on the banks of the Cocytus: "O Minos!" she cries, "O inexorable judge! I loved when on earth, it is true, I loved against the rigorous

125

laws of Vesta. If the gods are as barbarous as men, then let the depths of Tartarus engulf me! For I have loved, and I love still.'' ''—No, no, my child, you are not yet in the kingdom of the dead; come, poor thing, return to the earth! Return to the realm of light and love!'' Meanwhile I seize her hand, already cold with the chill of the grave; I lift her in my arms, pressed against my breast, and carry her away from that terrible place, her heart in a flutter from fear and gratitude.

Mind you, do not think, Madame, that any personal interest has motivated this good deed. The hope of winning the affections of the beautiful ex-vestal virgin enters not at all in anything I have done for her; for I should be thereby reverting to the former method: I can assure you, on my word as a traveller, that for the entire length of our walk from the Colline Gate to the spot where the tomb of the Scipios now lies, I never once, despite the darkness, not even in those moments when her weakness forced me to carry her in my arms, treated her with anything but the consideration and respect befitting her misfortunes. Indeed, I scrupulously returned her to her lover, who was waiting for her along the road.

CHAPTER XXV*

Another time, carried away by my reveries, I found myself by chance at the rape of the Sabine women: I was surprised to see that the Sabine men were reacting to the event in a manner entirely different from the historical account. Not knowing what to make of that free-for-all, I offered my protection to a fleeing woman; and as I accompanied her, I could not help but laugh when I heard a furious Sabine man cry out in despair: "Ye gods! Why did I not bring my wife to the party!"

CHAPTER XXVI

In addition to the half of the human race of which I am so terribly fond, I must say, believe it or not, that my heart's capacity for love is so great that all living beings and even inanimate objects enjoy their share of it as well. I love the trees that lend me their shade, and the birds that twitter amid the foliage, and the owl's nocturnal cry, and the sounds of the torrent: I love everything. . . . I love the moon!

You laugh, Mademoiselle: it is easy to make sport of feelings one does not share; but hearts like mine will understand.

Yes, I am bound by true affection to all that surrounds me. I love the roads on which I walk, I love the spring from which I drink: I can never part without sorrow from a stick I have extracted at random from a hedge; I keep looking at it after I have tossed it aside: we had already become acquainted. I regret the falling leaves, even the passing zephyr. Where is the wind that tousled your black hair, Elisa, when you sat beside me on the banks of the Doria on the eve of our eternal separation and looked at me in sorrowful silence? Where is your gaze? Where is that tearful, cherished moment?*

O time! Terrible divinity! It's not your cruel scythe that frightens me; I do not fear your hideous offspring, indifference and forgetting, which turn three fourths of our existence into one long death.

Alas! that zephyr, that gaze, that smile are as remote from me as Ariadne's adventures: at the bottom of my heart there remain but regrets and vain recollections, a miscellany of sadness on whose surface my life still floats, as a vessel devastated by the hurricane still floats for a time upon the stormy sea.

CHAPTER XXVII

—Until, the water having seeped bit by bit between the shattered planks, the wretched vessel sinks into the fathomless deep and disappears, and the waves roll over it, the storm subsides, and the sea swallow skims the calm and lonely plain of Ocean.

CHAPTER XXVIII

I'm afraid I must here terminate the explanation of my new method for making love, for I can see that it is ending up in gloom. It would not be inappropriate, however, to add a few more elucidations concerning this discovery, which is not universally suited to everyone, nor to every age of life. I should not advise anyone to put it into practice at the age of twenty. The inventor himself did not use it in that period of his life. To obtain the best possible results from it, one must have already experienced all of life's sorrows without losing heart, and all of its pleasures without losing one's taste for it. Not an easy thing! It is especially useful at that age when reason counsels us to give up the habits of youth, and may serve as an imperceptible passage, a bridge between pleasure and wisdom. This passage, as every moralist has observed, is a very difficult one. Few men have the noble courage to cross it valiantly, and often after they have taken that step, they grow bored on the other bank and cross back over the moat with grizzled hair and to their great shame. My new way of making love will spare them that tribulation. Indeed, since most of our pleasures are but the play of the imagination, it is essential to offer it some harmless food to distract it from the things we cannot have, just as we give toys to little children when we refuse them sweets. In this way one has the time to fortify oneself on wisdom's ground, without giving a thought to being there yet, and one arrives there by way of madness, which will make it particularly easy for a great many people to reach.

I therefore believe that I was not mistaken in my hope of being useful, which led me to take pen in hand; and I now need only refrain from the natural impulse of pride, which I might justifiably feel in unveiling such truths to humanity.

CHAPTER XXIX

The secrets I have just revealed to you, my dear Sophie, will not, I hope, have made you forget the awkward position in which you left me at my window. The excitement that the sight of my neighbor's dainty foot had stirred in me remained, and I was more than ever under the spell of the dangerous slipper, when an unforeseen occurrence rescued me from the danger I was in, to wit, that of plummeting five stories into the street. A bat that had been prowling about the building and, seeing me motionless for such a long time, must have taken me for a column or a chimney, suddenly swooped down on me and hung itself from my ear. I felt the ghastly chill of its wet wings against my cheek. Every echo in Turin answered the wild scream that escaped from me in spite of myself. The distant sentries sounded the alarm, and in the streets I heard the hurried steps of a patrol.

I abandoned the view of the balcony without much difficulty, since it no longer had any appeal for me. The night's chill had taken hold of me. A slight shiver ran through me from head to toe, and as I pulled my dressing gown tighter around me to warm up, I realized, to my great regret, that this feeling of cold, combined with the insult of the bat, had sufficed to change the course of my thoughts again. The magic slipper would not have had any more power over me at this moment than the Coma Berenices or any other constellation. I reckoned at once how foolish it was to pass the night exposed to the inclemency of the elements instead of obeying nature's command to sleep. My powers of reasoning, which at this moment were acting alone inside me, made me see this as clearly as if it were a Euclidian proposition. Suddenly I was bereft of imagination and inspiration, and abandoned to dreary reality without hope of recall. Deplorable existence! One might as well be a withered tree in the forest or an obelisk in the middle of a public square!

What a strange pair of machines, I exclaimed to myself, are man's head and heart! Swept away by turns in opposite directions by these two motors of his actions, he always believes the last one he has followed is the better! O folly of enthusiasm and sentiment! says cold reason; O weak, uncertain reason! says sentiment. Who will ever manage, who will ever dare decide between the two?

I thought it might be nice to resolve the matter then and there and decide once and for all to which of these two guides I should entrust myself for the rest of my life. Will I follow henceforth my head or my heart? Let us see.

CHAPTER XXX

In saying these words, I felt a dull pain in the foot that was resting on the step of the ladder. I was, moreover, very weary from the difficult position I had been holding until that moment. I lowered myself gently to sit down, and letting my legs hang to the right and left of the window, I began the horse-back part of my voyage. I have always preferred this manner of travel to all others, and I love horses with a passion: of all the horses I have seen or of which I have heard mention, however, the one I should most ardently have liked to own was the wooden horse that figures in *The Thousand and One Nights,* on whose back one could travel through the air, and which took off when one turned a little peg between its ears.

Now it may be observed that my steed is very much like the one in *The Thousand and One Nights*. From this position, the traveler astride his window can, to one side, look onto the sky and enjoy the imposing spectacle of nature: the stars and meteors are at his disposal; to the other side, the sight of his home and the objects in it recall his daily life to him and bring him back to himself. A mere movement of the head takes the place of the magic peg and suffices to effect, in the traveler's soul, a change as swift as it is unusual. Inhabiting the earth and the heavens by turns, his mind and heart pass through every delight of which man is capable.

I had an inkling beforehand of all the use I might get from my steed. Once I was snug in the saddle and as ready as I could be, certain of having nothing to fear from thieves or from a stumbling horse, I found the moment ripe for devoting my attentions to the question I had set for myself regarding the primacy of reason or sentiment. My first thought on the matter, however, stopped me short. Is it my place to declare myself judge in a case of this nature?—I said to myself under my breath. I who, deep down, have already decided in favor of sentiment?—On the other hand, if I exclude people for whom the heart outweighs the head, to whom could I turn? To a geometer? Bah! People like that have sold themselves to reason! To settle this matter, one would have to find a man who was by nature endowed with equal shares of reason and sentiment, and at the moment of decision these two faculties would have to be in perfect equilibrium—an impossibility! It would be easier to keep a republic in equilibrium.

The only competent judge would therefore be one who had nothing to do with the one or the other, a man, in short, without head or heart. This bizarre conclusion offended my reason; and my heart, in turn, protested having no part in it. Nevertheless, it seemed to me well reasoned, and I might, in this instance, have accepted the worst idea hatched by my intellect, had I not reflected that in speculations of high metaphysics, such as the one in question, first-rate philosophers have often, by following their arguments through to the end, arrived at frightful conclusions, which have had an effect on the welfare of human society. I took comfort in the thought that the outcome of my speculations at least would cause no harm to anyone. I therefore left the question undecided, and resolved for the rest of my days to follow alternately my head and my heart, depending on which had the upper hand. And I believe, in fact, that this is the best way. It has not, it is true, brought me great fortune thus far! No matter: I go down life's steep path without fear and without plans, laughing and weeping by turns, and often at once, or else whistling some old melody to amuse myself along the way. At other times I pick a daisy from the corner of a hedgerow and tear off the petals one by one, saying: "She loves me, she loves me not, she loves me, she loves me not . . ." The last one almost always ends with *she loves me not*. And in fact, Elisa no longer loves me.

While busying myself thus, an entire generation of the living passes by like a tremendous wave about to break with me against eternity's shore; and as if the storm of life were not violent enough, as if it were pushing us too slowly toward the barriers of existence, nations rush to butcher one another wholesale and anticipate the end decreed by nature. Conquerers, themselves borne along by time's swift whirlwind, take their pleasure by sending thousands into eternity. Hey, gentlemen! What is the meaning of this? Wait! These good people were all going to die a natural death. Do you not see the wave approaching? It's already foaming close to shore. . . . Wait, for heaven's sake, just a moment longer, and you, and your enemies, and I and the daisies, shall all come to an end! Does such lunacy ever cease to amaze! Well, then! the matter is settled: from this time forth I will no longer pluck the petals from daisies.

Chapter XXXI

Having set for myself a rule of prudent conduct for the future through the sort of brilliant logic that we have encountered in the preceding chapters, there remained one important matter for me to settle concerning the journey I was about to undertake. It is not, indeed, enough to hop into the carriage or onto the horse's back: one must also know where it is that one wishes to go. I was so weary from the metaphysical inquiries with which I had been lately occupied that, before deciding upon which region of the globe I should prefer, I wanted to rest a while and think of nothing whatsoever. It is a manner of existence also of my own invention, one from which I have often derived great benefits; yet not everyone can turn it to account: for if it is easy to deepen one's ideas by applying oneself vigorously to a subject, it is not so easy to stop one's thought all at once the way one stops a pendulum! Molière was quite wrong to poke fun at the man who amused himself making circles in a well; I myself am inclined to believe that this man was a philosopher who had the power to suspend the activity of his intelligence in order to rest, one of the most difficult procedures for the human mind to carry out. I know that those who were given this ability without having desired it, and who as a rule are never thinking of anything, will accuse me of plagiarism and demand credit for the invention; yet the state of intellectual immobility whereof I speak is different in nature from the sort they enjoy, of which M. Necker has written an apologia.* Mine is always voluntary and can only be of brief duration; to enjoy it in all its fullness, I closed my eyes while leaning with my hands against the window as a weary horseman leans against the pommel of the saddle, and soon the memory of the past, the sense of the present, and the presentiment of the future all vanished in my soul.

As this mode of existence strongly favors the onset of sleep, after half a minute of enjoyment I felt my head nod: opening my eyes at once, my thoughts resumed their train—which clearly proves that the sort of voluntary lethargy in question is quite different from sleep, since I was wakened by sleep itself, something which I am sure has never happened to anyone else.

Raising my eyes to the heavens, I noticed the polestar over the ridge of the roof, and this seemed to me a rather good omen at a moment when I was about to embark on a long journey. During the interval of rest that I had just enjoyed, my imagination had regained all its strength and my heart was now ready to receive the sweetest of impressions—so greatly is its energy increased by that momentary annihilation of thought. The sense of distress that my precarious situation in the world caused me secretly to feel was at once replaced by a keen sense of hope and optimism; I now felt capable of confronting life and all the chances for misfortune and happiness that trail behind in its wake.

Bright shining orb!—I exclaimed, transported by my ecstasy. Unfathomable product of eternal thought! You who, since the day of creation, immobile in the heavens, alone keep watch over one half of the earth! You who guide the navigator over the deserts of the Ocean, and from whom a single glance has often revived the hopes and the very life of a sailor pressed hard by a storm! If I have never failed, when a clear night let me contemplate the heavens, to seek you out among your companions, succor me now, celestial beacon! The earth, alas! has abandoned me: be my counsel and my guide, show me in what region of the globe I should dwell!

During this invocation, the star seemed to beam

more radiantly and to rejoice in the sky, inviting me to come under its protective influence.

I do not believe in omens; but I do believe in a divine providence that guides men by unknown means. Every instant of our existence is a new creation, an act of all-powerful will. The changeable order that produces the ever new forms and inexplicable marvels of clouds is at every moment predetermined down to the tiniest particle of water composing them: the events of our lives themselves could not have any other cause, and to attribute them to chance would be the height of folly. I can even assert that I have happened at times to catch a glimpse of the imperceptible strings by which Providence guides the actions of the most powerful men like marionettes, while they themselves imagine they are leading the world; a little fit of pride, breathed into their hearts, is enough to send whole armies to their deaths, or to turn a nation upside down. Be that as it may, I believed so firmly in the invitation I had received from the polestar that on the spot my mind was made up to go north; and although I had no point of preference or specific destination in those distant regions, when I left Turin the following day I left by way of the Palace Gate solely because it is at the northern end of the city, convinced that the polestar would not abandon me.

CHAPTER XXXII

I had come this far in my journey when I was
forced to dismount. I should not even have mentioned this detail if I did not feel, in all good conscience, that I must inform those who would adopt
this new manner of travel of the minor inconveniences it may present, having already demonstrated
its tremendous advantages.

Since windows, generally speaking, were not
originally invented for the new purpose I have given
them, the architects who construct them usually neglect to give them the rounded, comfortable form of
an English saddle. The intelligent reader, I trust, will
understand without further explantion the painful
cause of my need to make a stop at this point in my
journey. I dismounted with some difficulty, then
walked back and forth several times lengthwise
across my room to restore the circulation, reflecting upon the mix of pains and pleasures with which
life is sprinkled, as well as on the sort of fate
that enslaves a man to the most insignificant circumstances. Whereafter I hastened to remount my horse,
equipped with an eiderdown pillow—which I should
never have dared attempt only a few days before, for
fear of being jeered by the cavalry; but, having encountered the previous day, at the gates of Turin, a
party of Cossacks who had come all the way from
the Palus Maeotis* and the Caspian Sea on similar
pillows, I decided that I could, without violating the

rules of horsemanship, for which I have great respect, adopt the same practice.

Now free of the unpleasant sensation to which I
discreetly alluded above, I could turn to my travel
plans with an untroubled mind.

One of the problems that bothered me most, since
it concerned my conscience, was that of knowing
whether I was right or wrong in abandoning my
country, half of which had abandoned me herself.*
A decision of this nature seemed to me too important
to take lightly. Turning that word, "country," over
in my mind, I realized I did not have a very clear idea
of its meaning.—My country? What constitutes a
country? Is it a collection of houses, fields, rivers? I
should not think so. Perhaps my country is where my
family and friends are? But they've already abandoned it. Ah, that must be it: it's the government—
but that's been changed. God almighty! Where,
then, is my country? I wiped my brow with my hand,
in a state of indescribable agitation. The love of
one's country is so exacting! The regrets I felt at the
mere thought of abandoning my own so well proved
its existence that I would have remained on horse-
back for the rest of my life rather than quit before
having settled this problem once and for all.

I soon realized that love of one's country depends
upon a combination of several factors: to wit, the
long familiarity that man, from childhood, gains
with the people, the place, and the government.
Now it was only a question of examining in what

respects these three elements contribute, each in its way, to making up a country.

One's attachment to one's countrymen usually depends on the government and is nothing more than a sense of the power and well-being that it gives to us all; for true attachment is limited to the family and to a small number of individuals from our immediate surroundings. Everything that comes between customs, or makes it difficult for men to meet, turns them into enemies: a mountain chain creates ultramontanes on both sides who don't like one another; the inhabitants of the right bank of a river think themselves quite superior to those of the left bank, and the latter make fun of their neighbors in turn. This tendency can be seen even in large cities divided by a river, despite the bridges uniting its banks. Differences of language go even further toward dividing men under the same government. Finally, the family itself, in which we invest our truest affections, is often scattered about a country; it is continually changing in form and number; moreover, it can be transported. Therefore it is neither in our countrymen nor in our families that the love of country fundamentally resides.

The place contributes at least as much to the attachment we feel toward our native land. And here a most interesting question arises. It has always been said that highlanders are of all people the most attached to their country, and that nomadic people usually inhabit the great plains. What could be the reason for this difference in these people's attachment to their localities? If I am not mistaken, it is as follows: in the highlands, the country has a physiognomy; in the plains, it has none. It's a faceless woman one could never love, despite all her good qualities. Indeed, what is left of a village of wooden houses after the enemy passes through, burns down the town, and fells all the trees? In vain the unhappy villager looks about, over the flat line of the horizon, for some familiar object that might evoke memories: none whatsoever remains. Every point in space presents the same sight, the same concern. This man is nomadic by necessity, unless the habit of governance restrains him; but he will dwell in one place or another, it makes no difference; his country is wherever his government is practiced: he will never have but half a country. The highlander, on the other hand, is attached to things he has had before his eyes since childhood, things which have visible, indestructible forms: from every point in the valley below, he can see and recognize his field on the hillside. The sound of the stream bubbling between the rocks has never stopped; the path leading to the village bends around an immutable granite boulder. In his dreams he sees the outline of the mountains painted in his heart, just as we, after looking a long time at a latticed window, continue to see the partitions when we close our eyes: the picture etched in his memory is part of him, and will never fade.

In short, memories themselves are related to

place, but the place must contain things whose origins are unknown and whose end cannot be foreseen. Ancient edifices, old bridges, all that bears the stamp of greatness and longevity can in part replace the role of mountains in people's fondness for place; natural monuments, however, have greater power over the human heart. To give Rome an appellation worthy of her, the proud Romans called her *the City of Seven Hills*. Once acquired, the habit cannot be broken. The highlander, in his later years, can no longer grow fond of the places in a large city, and the city dweller could never become a highlander. This perhaps explains why one of the greatest writers of our time, whose talents brought the fascination of the American wilderness to our attention, found the Alps rather paltry, and Mont Blanc considerably too small.*

The role of government is clear: it is a country's foundation stone, upon which all else rests. It creates people's attachment to one another, and gives strength to their natural attachment to the place; it alone, through memories of happiness or glory, can bind them to the soil that they have known from birth.

If the government is good, the country is at the peak of health; if it becomes corrupt, the country takes ill; if it changes, the country dies. It becomes a new country, and each is free to embrace it or to choose another.

When the entire population of Athens quit that

city on the strength of Themistocles' word, did they abandon their country? Or did they take it with them onto their ships?*

When Coriolanus . . .

Good heavens! What sort of discussion have I entered into? I forget that I am straddling my window.

CHAPTER XXXIII

I once had an old aunt who was a great wit and whose conversations were always very interesting; her memory, however, at once erratic and rich, would often lead her from one episode to another, and from one digression to another, to the point that she had to ask for help from her listeners: ''What was it I wanted to tell you?'' she used to say, and oftentimes her listeners themselves had forgotten, which then threw everyone present into an unspeakable state of confusion. Now, it has been observed that the same sort of accident often happens to me in my narrations, and I must indeed admit that the plan and order of my journey are exact copies of the order and plan of my aunt's conversations. Yet I require no assistance from anyone, for I have noticed that my subject always comes back by itself, at the moment when I least expect it.

CHAPTER XXXIV

Those who will disapprove of my disquisition on the love of country should be informed that sleep, by then, had been gaining on me for some time, despite the efforts I made to fight it. Now, however, I am not quite sure whether or not I fell asleep in earnest, nor whether the extraordinary things I am about to relate were the product of a dream or of a supernatural vision.

I saw a bright cloud descend from the sky and slowly draw near to me; inside it, covered as with a transparent veil, was a young woman of twenty-two or twenty-three years. It would be useless to look for expressions to describe the emotion I felt upon beholding her. Her countenance, radiating goodness and benevolence, was as enchanting as the illusions of youth and sweet as the dreams of the future; her gaze, her serene smile, all her features, in fact, embodied to my eyes the ideal being that my heart had been seeking for so long, and that I had despaired of ever encountering.

As I contemplated her in my delicious ecstasy, I saw the polestar twinkle amidst the curls of her black hair, which the north wind gently tousled, and at that moment I heard some comforting words. Words? No, no: it was the mysterious expression of divine thought unveiling the future to my intelligence while my senses were paralyzed by sleep; it was a prophetic message from the favorable star I had lately invoked, whose meaning I will now endeavor to express in a human tongue.

"Your faith in me will not be betrayed," said a voice whose timbre was like the sound of Aeolian harps. "Look: behold the companion I have chosen for you; behold the goodness yearned for in vain by men who believe that happiness can be planned, and who demand of the earth what can only be had from heaven." With these words, the meteor returned to the depths of the heavens, the airy divinity vanished in the mists of the horizon; yet as she withdrew she cast a glance at me that filled my heart with faith and hope.

At once, burning to follow her, I spurred my horse with all my might, but, as I had forgotten to put on spurs, I struck my right heel so hard against the corner of a tile that the pain woke me up with a start.

This accident proved a real boon to the geological part of my journey, for it gave me an opportunity to learn exactly how high my room was above the alluvial deposits that make up the soil on which the city of Turin is built.

My heart was racing fast, and I had just counted three and a half beats from the moment I had spurred my horse, when I heard the sound of my slipper falling into the street, which, taking into account the amount of time it takes for a heavy body to fall according to the acceleration of gravity and the time needed for the sound waves to travel from the street up to my ear, puts the height of my window at ninety-four feet, three lines, and nine-tenths of a line* from the level of the pavement of Turin, assuming that my heart, excited by the dream, was beating one hundred twenty times per minute, which cannot be too far from the truth. Of course, it is only from a scientific point of view that, after having spoken of the enchanting slipper of my lovely neighbor, I dare make any mention of my own. And I hasten to add that this chapter is intended strictly for scientists.

CHAPTER XXXV

The dazzling vision I had just experienced made me feel all the more keenly, upon awaking, the horror of the isolation in which I found myself. I looked all around me and saw nothing but roofs and chimneys. Alas! Suspended five stories high between sky and earth, surrounded by an ocean of regrets, desires, and troubles, I clung to life only by an uncertain glimmer of hope—a fanciful support at best, the fragility of which was all too familiar to me. Doubt soon returned to my heart, which was still broken from life's disappointments, and I truly believed that the polestar had made fun of me. O unjust and blameworthy defiance, for which the orb punished me by making me wait ten years! If only I had foreseen that all its promises would be kept and that one day I would find on earth the venerated creature whose image I had merely glimpsed in the heavens! Dear Sophie, if only I had known that my happiness would exceed my wildest hopes! . . . But I must not get ahead of myself: I will return to my subject, as I do not wish to reverse the methodical and rigorous order that I have been following in drafting this account of my journey.

CHAPTER XXXVI

The clock on the belfry of Saint-Philippe slowly tolled midnight. I counted each peal of the bell, one after the other, and the last ring drew a sigh from my breast. ''And so another day departs my life,'' I said to myself, ''and while the diminishing vibrations of the resounding brass still tremble in my ear, that part of my journey that preceded midnight is already as remote from me as the voyages of Ulysses or Jason. In the abyss of the past, instants and centuries are equal in length—and is the future any more real? They are two voids between which I stand poised as on the edge of a blade. In truth, time seems so inconceivable to me that I am almost tempted to believe that it doesn't actually exist, and that the thing that we call time is but a punishment of the mind.''

I was rejoicing in having come up with this definition of time, as sombre as time itself, when another clock struck midnight, which gave me a singularly unpleasant feeling. There always remains a residue of gloom inside me after I have been uselessly occupied in trying to solve an insoluble problem, and I found it quite out of place that this second belfry should make such an announcement to a philosopher like me. But I felt downright resentful when a few seconds later, a third bell tower, that of the Capuchin monastery, on the opposite bank of the Po, once again chimed midnight, as if out of spite.

When my aunt used to call for her old housemaid, a cantankerous woman of whom she was nevertheless rather fond, she was never content, in her impatience, to ring just once; rather, she would pull on the bell without respite until the maid appeared. "Come on, Mademoiselle Branchet!" she would say. And the other, irritated at being rushed in this manner, would say quite bitterly, before entering the room: "Coming, Madame, coming." The ill humor I felt upon hearing the impudent bell tower of the Capuchins strike twelve for the third time was exactly the same. "I know, I know," I cried out, holding my hands out to the clock, "I know indeed that it is midnight, I know it only too well."

It must undoubtedly have been at the insidious urging of the Evil One that men appointed this hour to divide their days. Shut inside their homes, they are asleep or amusing themselves while it severs another thread of their lives: the next day they rise cheerfully, without suspecting in the least that they are one day older. In vain does the prophetic voice of the brass announce the approach of eternity, in vain does it gloomily repeat to them each hour that passes; they hear nothing, or if they do hear, they do not understand. O midnight! Dreadful hour! I am not superstitious, but that hour has always inspired a kind of terror in me, and I have a premonition that, if I were to die, it would be at midnight.—So I, too, shall die one day? What! I, die? I who speak, who can feel and touch myself: Could I really die? I have some difficulty believing this: because others, of course, die, nothing could be more natural; we see it every day, we see them pass away, we grow accustomed to it: but to die oneself! to die personally!— that's a bit much. And you, gentlemen, you who take these wise reflections for gibberish, be assured that everyone in the world thinks this way, yourselves included. Nobody thinks that he has to die one day. And if there existed a race of immortal men, the idea of death would terrify them even more than us.

There is something in this I don't quite understand, however. How is it that humans, who are forever stirred by the hopes and illusions of the future, worry so little about the only sure and inevitable thing this future has to offer? Might it not be beneficent nature herself who gave us this happy insouciance, that we might fulfill our destiny in peace? Indeed, I believe that one can be a perfectly respectable man without augmenting life's real woes with this turn of mind, which leads to dark thoughts, and without disturbing one's fancy with morbid phantoms. In short, I think that one must dare to laugh, or at least to smile, every time the innocent occasion arises.

Thus ended the meditation that the bells of Saint-Philippe had inspired in me. I would have carried it further, had I not had some misgivings as to the severity of the moral I had just proposed. However, having no desire to get to the bottom of this doubt, I whistled the melody to the *Folies d'Espagne,** which has the ability to change the direction of my thoughts when they go astray. It so quickly achieved the desired effect that I terminated my ride then and there.

CHAPTER XXXVII

Before going back into my room, I cast a glance over the city of Turin and its dark countryside, which I was soon to leave, perhaps forever, and I said my final good-bys to them. Never had the night looked so beautiful; never had the sight before my eyes so enchanted me. After giving my regards to the mountain and the temple of the Superga, I took my leave of the towers, belfries, and all those familiar objects whose loss I never dreamed I could mourn so deeply—the air and the sky, and the river whose hushed murmur seemed to return my good-bys. Ah, if only I knew how to paint the sweet yet cruel sensation that filled my heart, and all the memories of the better, bygone half of my life that crowded round me like sprites to make me stay in Turin! But, alas! memories of past happiness are the soul's wrinkles. When you are sad, you must chase them from your mind like ghosts who return to mock our present situation: it's a thousand times better to abandon oneself to deceptive illusions of hope; and one must, above all, smile in the face of adversity and take good care not to confide one's sorrows to anyone. I have observed, in my ordinary travels among human beings, that too much unhappiness makes one ridiculous in the end. In these dreadful moments, nothing is more helpful than the new manner of travel of which you have just read the description. My experience was decisive: not only did I succeed in forgetting the past, but I was able to make the best of my present troubles. Time will bear them away, I said to console myself; it takes everything and forgets nothing as it passes; and whether we try to stop it or give it, so to speak, a nudge of the shoulder, our efforts are equally vain and do nothing to alter its inexorable march. Though in general I worry myself very little about its swiftness, there are certain circumstances, certain trains of thought that recall it suddenly to my mind. When people fall silent, when the Demon of noise is hushed at the heart of his temple, in the heart of a sleeping city, that is when time raises its voice for my soul to hear it. Silence and darkness become its interpreters and reveal to me its mysterious workings; no longer a creature of reason that my mind cannot grasp, it is something I perceive directly with my senses. I see it in the sky, driving the stars westward. And there it is, pushing the rivers to the sea and rolling down the hillside with the fog.—I listen: the winds moan under the strain of its swiftly beating wings, and the distant belfry howls in its ghostly path.

"Let us take advantage of its passing," I cried. "I

will use every moment to the full before it snatches them away from me." Wishing thus to turn this resolution to account, I leaned forward to spring bravely into action, making certain clucking sounds with my tongue which since time immemorial have served to urge horses on, but which are impossible to write according to the rules of spelling:

kh! kh! kh!

and so I ended my ride with a good gallop.

CHAPTER XXXVIII

As I was raising my right leg to dismount, I felt myself struck rather hard on the shoulder. To say I was not startled by this unexpected occurrence would be to trifle with the truth; and this is an excellent moment to bring to the reader's attention, and to prove to him, with due modesty, of course, how difficult it would be for anyone but me to undertake a voyage of this nature. Even supposing the new voyager to possess a thousand times the means and talents of observation that I have, could he ever hope to know adventures so extraordinary and numerous as those that befell me in the space of four hours, and which are clearly part of my destiny? If anyone has any doubts about this, let him try to guess who just struck me!

In my initial confusion, not considering the situation I was in, I thought perhaps my horse had given a kick or knocked me against a tree. God only knows how many ominous ideas rushed into my head in the brief amount of time that it took me to turn my head to look into the room. At that moment I saw, as often happens in matters that seem the most extraordinary, that the cause of my surprise was perfectly natural. The same gust of wind that at the beginning of my journey had opened my window and shut my door in passing, one part of which had slipped between the curtains of my bed, was now blowing back into my room with a great uproar; it opened the door abruptly and left through the window, pushing the pane against my shoulder, which gave me the surprise I have just mentioned.

One will recall that it was at the invitation of this puff of wind that I had risen from my bed. The jolt I had just received was obviously an invitation to return there, and I felt obliged to accept.

It is wonderful, of course, to enjoy such familiar relations with the night, the heavens, and meteors, and to know how to benefit from their influence. The relations we are forced to have with our fellow men are so much more dangerous! How often I've been fooled by my trust in those fine gentlemen! I even said something on this matter in a note here, but I have suppressed it, for the note turned out to be longer than the entire text, and that would have spoiled the excellent proportions of my journey, whose brevity is its greatest merit.*

THE LEPER OF
THE CITY OF AOSTA
(1811)

Ah! little thinck the gay licentious proud,
Whom pleasure, power and affluence surround . . .
Ah! little thinck they, while they dance along . . .
How many pine!... how many drinck the cup
Of baleful grief!... how many shake
With all the fiercer tortures of the mind!

(Thompson's Seasons, *The Winter*)

The southern part of the city of Aosta is almost deserted, and seems never to have been greatly populated. One sees ploughed fields there, and meadows bordered on one side by the ancient ramparts erected by the Romans to serve as the city's enceinte, and on the other side by the walls of a few gardens. This solitary site may, however, be of interest to travelers. Near the city's gate stand the ruins of an ancient castle, in which in the fifteenth century, according to popular legend, the Count René de Chalans, in a jealous fury, allowed the Princess Marie de Bragance, his wife, to die of hunger. Hence the name of *Bramafan* (which means *cry of hunger*) given the castle by the local people. This anecdote, whose authenticity might well be questioned, lends meaning to those vestiges for the sensitive souls who believe it to be true.

Farther on, a few hundred paces away, is a square tower abutting the ancient wall and built of the same marble that once covered it: it is called *The Tower of Fright,* for the people long believed it to be inhabited by ghosts. The old wives of the city of Aosta can still remember having seen emerge from there, on gloomy nights, a tall, white woman holding a lamp in her hand.

About fifteen years ago, this tower was restored by order of the governor and surrounded by a wall, for the purpose of housing a leper and keeping him apart from human society, while offering him all the amenities that his sad condition might allow him. The hospice of Saint-Maurice was charged with seeing to his needs, and provided him with some articles of furniture and the tools necessary for cultivating a garden. He had been living there a long time, left to himself, never seeing anyone save the priest who came from time to time to offer him the solace of religion and the man who each week brought him his provisions from the hospice, when in 1797, during the Alpine War, a soldier, finding himself in the city of Aosta, happened to pass by the leper's garden, which in his curiosity he entered. There he found a man in simple dress, leaning against a tree and absorbed in deep meditation. At the sound the officer made upon entering, the recluse, without turning around or looking, cried out in a sorrowful voice: *Who goes there, and what does he want of me?*— Please excuse a stranger who may have been prompted to commit an indiscretion by the sight your lovely garden, replied the soldier; he has no wish to disturb you. *Come no closer,* replied the inhabitant of the tower with a gesture of his hand, *come no closer; you are in the presence of a wretch afflicted with leprosy.*—Whatever your misfortune, replied the traveler, I will not withdraw; I have never shunned the unfortunate. Yet if my presence disturbs you, I am ready to leave.

Welcome, then, said the leper, turning suddenly about; *you may stay, if you dare, after you have seen me.* The soldier froze for a moment in astonishment and fright at the sight of that unhappy man, whom leprosy had entirely disfigured.—I shall be glad to stay, he said, if you don't mind a visit from a man brought here by chance, yet kept here by the keenest of interest.

THE LEPER

Interest! . . . I've never aroused anything but pity.

THE SOLDIER

I should think myself happy if I could offer you some consolation.

THE LEPER

It is a great consolation for me just to see my fellow men and to hear the sound of the human voice, which seems to shun me.

THE SOLDIER

Allow me then to converse with you a few moments, and to have a look around your home.

THE LEPER

With pleasure, if that is your wish. (In saying these words, the leper covered his head with a broad felt hat with the brim turned down to hide his face.) Come this way, he added; here to the south, I tend a bed of flowers you might find to your liking; you will find some rather rare varieties. I obtained seeds from all the flowers growing wild in the Alps and have tried to cultivate them here and enhance their beauty with care.

THE SOLDIER

Indeed, I've never seen flowers like these in all
my life.

THE LEPER

Look at this little rosebush: it's the rose without thorns, and grows only high up in the Alps.
But already it has begun to lose that property, and
grows thorns the more it is cultivated and multi-
plies.

THE SOLDIER

It must be the very image of ingratitude.

THE LEPER

If any of these flowers strike you as beautiful, you
may take them without fear; you run no risk carrying
them on your person. I planted them and have the
pleasure of watering them and looking at them; but I
never touch them.

THE SOLDIER

Why not?

THE LEPER

I am afraid of tainting them, and then I could
never give them away.

THE SOLDIER

To whom do you give them?

THE LEPER

The people who bring me my provisions from the
hospice are not afraid to make bouquets of them.

Sometimes even the children from town appear at my garden gate, and I climb up into my tower at once, lest I should frighten them or bring them harm. From my window, I watch them frolic about and make off with some of my flowers. As they leave, they look up at me: *Good day, leper,* they say to me laughing, and it cheers me up a little.

THE SOLDIER

You have managed to bring together a great many different plants here; I see vines and fruit trees of diverse species.

THE LEPER

The trees are still young. I planted them myself, and this vine too: I've made it climb to the top of the ancient wall you see there, which serves me as a little walkway. It's my favorite place . . . Climb up these stones here: they form a stairway of which I myself am the architect. Hold on to the wall.

THE SOLDIER

What a charming spot! And quite suitable for the meditations of a solitary man.

THE LEPER

I too like it very much: from here I can see the countryside and the laborers in the fields. I see everything that goes on in the meadow below, and am seen by no one.

THE SOLDIER

I marvel at the peace and solitude of this retreat. We are in a city, and yet one would think we were in the wild.

THE LEPER

Solitude is not always found in the middle of the forest or among the rocks. The unhappy man is everywhere alone.

THE SOLDIER

What sequence of events led you to this retreat? Is this country your home?

THE LEPER

I was born by the sea, in the principality of Oneglia, and have lived here but fifteen years. As for my story, it has been nothing but one long and endless calamity.

THE SOLDIER

Have you always lived alone?

THE LEPER

I lost my parents during infancy and never knew them. The one sister left to me died two years ago. I have never had a friend.

THE SOLDIER

Unlucky man!

THE LEPER

Such are God's designs.

THE SOLDIER

What is your name, if I may ask?

THE LEPER

Oh! It's a terrible name! I am called *The Leper!*
Nobody knows what name I inherited from my
family or what name I was given by my religion at
birth. I am *The Leper:* it is my only claim to the
benevolence of others. May they never know who I
am!

THE SOLDIER

The sister you lost, did she live with you?

THE LEPER

She lived with me for five years, in the same
abode in which you find me now. As wretched as I,
she shared my afflictions, and I tried to lessen her
own.

THE SOLDIER

How do you occupy your time now, living in a
solitude so deep?

THE LEPER

The story of the occupations of a hermit such as I
could only bore a man of the world who finds his
happiness in social activities.

Alas! how little you know that world, which has never given me any happiness at all. Indeed, I often choose to be alone; our ideas are perhaps more similar than you think. All the same, I must admit that the thought of eternal solitude terrifies me. I have trouble even conceiving it.

THE LEPER

He who cherishes his cell shall find peace therein. The imitation of Jesus Christ teaches us so. I am beginning to learn how true these consoling words are. The feeling of loneliness is also alleviated by work. A man who works is never entirely unhappy: I am proof of that. During the summer months, I have enough to keep me busy cultivating my garden and my flower bed; in winter, I make baskets and mats; I make my own clothes, cook my own food with the provisions brought to me from the hospice, and fill the remaining hours with prayer. In the end, the year goes by, and once it is past, it actually seems to have been rather brief.

THE SOLDIER

It must seem like a century to you.

THE LEPER

Pain and sorrow make the hours seem long, yet the years always fly by with the same speed. There is also, at the final limit of misfortune, a joy that the common run of men cannot know, and which will seem to you rather odd: the joy of existing and breathing. During the summer months, I spend whole days sitting motionless on this rampart, enjoying the air and the beauties of nature. All my thoughts become vague, indistinct; sorrow rests within my heart but does not overwhelm it; my gaze wanders across the countryside and the rocks surrounding us. All these different sights are so impressed in my memory that they have become, so to speak, part of me; each place is a friend whom I see every day with great pleasure.

THE SOLDIER

I have often felt something similar. When sorrow weighs heavy on me, and I do not find in men's hearts what my own heart desires, the sight of nature and inanimate things consoles me; I feel affection for the rocks and trees, and all the creatures on earth seem like friends given to me by God.

THE LEPER

You embolden me to recount to you in turn what stirs within me. I truly love those things that are, so to speak, my life's companions, and which I see every day. Every evening, before retiring to the tower, I come here to bid good night to the glaciers of Ruitorts, the dark woods of Mont Saint-Bernard, and the odd peaks dominating the Rhême valley. Although God's power is as visible in the creation of an ant as in the creation of the entire universe, the great spectacle of the mountains makes a greater impression on my senses: I can never look at those enormous shapes covered with eternal ice without a feeling of religious awe. And yet in the vast tableau surrounding me, I have my favorite sites which I love more than others; among them is the hermitage that you see up there, at the summit of Charvensod mountain. Isolated in the middle of a wood, near a secluded meadow, it receives the last rays of the setting sun. When evening falls, I sit in my garden and turn my gaze to that solitary hermitage, and my imagination finds rest there. It has become a kind of property to me; I have a vague sort of recollection of having lived there long ago, in happer times, the memory of which has faded from my mind. I especially love to contemplate the faraway mountains that blend into the sky on the horizon. Distance, like the future, awakens a feeling of hope in me: my despondent heart believes that there perhaps exists a very remote land where, in some future time, I shall at last be able to taste the happiness for which I yearn, which some secret intuition forever tells me is attainable.

THE SOLDIER

With so ardent a soul as yours, it must have taken a great deal of effort to resign yourself to your fate, and to keep from succumbing to despair.

THE LEPER

I should be deceiving you if I had you think I am always resigned to my lot. I have not attained the sort of self-abnegation that certain anchorites achieve. That total sacrifice of all human attachment still eludes me: my life is an unending series of struggles, and not even the powerful solace of religion can always stem the flights of my fancy. It often carries me away, in spite of myself, into an ocean of chimerical desires, which all lead me back to this world of which I haven't the slightest conception, yet whose fantastical image is ever present to torment me.

THE SOLDIER

If I could make you read what is in my heart, and convey to you the sense I have of this world, all your desires and regrets would vanish at once.

THE LEPER

A number of books have told me of man's perversity and the sorrows inseparable from humanity, but to no avail: my heart refuses to believe them. I always imagine gatherings of sincere and virtuous friends, or well-matched couples blessed with the happiness of health, youth, and good fortune. I picture them wandering together through greener, fresher groves than those that afford me shade, bathed in the light of a brighter sun than the one that shines on me, and their lot seems to me all the more enviable as my own is miserable. In early spring, when the Piedmont wind blows down into our valley, I feel imbued with its invigorating warmth, and I shudder in spite of myself. I experience a strange desire and a confused feeling of great happiness that could be mine to enjoy, were it not refused me. And so I flee my cell and wander about the countryside to breathe more freely. I avoid being seen by the very same people whom I am burning to meet; and from the top of the hill, hidden amidst the brush like a wild beast, I turn my eyes upon the city of Aosta. From afar, with envious eyes, I watch its inhabitants, who scarcely know me; I hold out my hands to them, sighing, and ask them for my share of happiness. In my rapture I have even—dare I say?—I have even held the trees of the forest in my arms, praying God to bring them to life for me, to give me a friend! But the trees remain silent; their cold bark spurns me; it has nothing in common with my burning, throbbing heart. Overwhelmed with fatigue, weary of life, I drag myself back to my retreat, present my torments to God, and prayer restores a little peace to my soul.

THE SOLDIER
Poor fellow! So you suffer all the ills of soul and body at once!

THE LEPER
The latter are not the cruelest!

THE SOLDIER
So they do give you respite sometimes?

THE LEPER
They grow and diminish each month in accordance with the phases of the moon. When it first

begins to appear, I usually suffer more; the illness then subsides and seems to change in nature: my skin dries up and turns white, and I hardly feel my affliction at all. Yet it would be tolerable at all times, if not for the terrible insomnia it causes me.

THE SOLDIER

What! Even sleep abandons you?

THE LEPER

Ah, insomnia! Sir, you cannot imagine how long and sad a night spent without shutting one's wretched eyes can be, when one's mind remains fixed on a frightful present and a future without hope! No, nobody can understand it. My worries increase as the night advances, and when it nears its end, so great is my restlessness I no longer know what to do with myself: my thoughts become blurred, and I experience an extraordinary feeling that only comes over me in these dark moments. At first, I feel as if an irresistible force is dragging me into a bottomless abyss; then I see black spots before my eyes; yet as I examine them, they begin to overlap with lightning speed, then they grow in size as they come closer and closer, and soon they are great mountains pressing down on me with their weight. At other times, I see clouds rise up from the earth around me, like great billows swelling up and threatening to engulf me, and when I try to rise to take my mind off these ideas, I feel as though restrained by invisible bonds, which rob me of my strength. You

169

will think perhaps that these are dreams. They are not, for I am quite awake. I see always the same things, and the terror I feel exceeds all my other afflictions.

THE SOLDIER

Perhaps you have a fever during these cruel bouts of insomnia, and that is the cause of this sort of delirium.

THE LEPER

Do you think that could come from a fever? Oh! May what you say be true! Until now I had feared these visions were a symptom of madness; and I confess, it troubled me greatly. Would to God it were indeed a fever!

THE SOLDIER

You interest me greatly. I must confess, I could never have imagined a situation such as yours. But I suppose it must have been less melancholy when your sister was alive.

THE LEPER

God alone knows what I lost when my sister died.—But are you not afraid to come so close to me? Please sit over here, on this stone; I shall go behind the foliage, and we can converse without seeing each other.

THE SOLDIER

Why, pray? No, you'll not leave my presence; rather, come sit here near me. (In saying these

170

words, the traveler made an involuntary movement to grasp the leper's hand, which the latter withdrew emphatically.)

THE LEPER

Imprudent man! You were going to grasp my hand!

THE SOLDIER

So I was! I would have clasped it with all my heart.

THE LEPER

It would have been the first time such a pleasure were granted me. I have never shaken hands with anyone.

THE SOLDIER

Really! So, but for the sister of whom you spoke, you have never had any intimate contact, have never been cherished by any of your fellow creatures?

THE LEPER

Fortunately for humanity, I have no fellow creatures.

THE SOLDIER

You make me shudder!

THE LEPER

Forgive me, compassionate stranger! You must know that the wretched like to speak of their misfortunes.

Oh, do speak, interesting man! You said that your sister used to live with you, and helped you to bear your sufferings.

She was the sole bond still linking me to the rest of humanity! It pleased God to break that bond, and to leave me isolated and alone in the world. Her soul was worthy of the heavens that now possess it; her example gave me sustenance against despondency, which often overcomes me now, since her death. We did not, however, live in that sweet intimacy which I can only imagine, and which must bring unhappy friends closer. The nature of our afflictions deprived us of that consolation. Even when we came together to pray to God, we used to avoid looking at each other, lest the sight of our afflictions might disturb our meditations; our eyes dared no longer meet except in heaven. After our prayers, my sister would customarily retire to her cell or go to sit under the hazel trees at the end of the garden. We lived almost entirely separate from each other.

But why impose such a harsh constraint on yourselves?

When my sister fell ill with the contagious disease of which my whole family was victim, and came to share my seclusion, we had never seen each other before. She had a terrible fright when she saw me for the first time. The fear of distressing her, and the even greater fear of aggravating her illness by coming close to her, forced me to adopt this sad manner of life. The leprosy had only attacked her chest, and I still harbored some hope of seeing her recover. Do you see this fragment of trellis that I have abandoned? At the time, it was a hedgerow of hops that I carefully tended and which divided the garden into two parts. I had fashioned a little path on either side of it, along which we could stroll and converse together without seeing or coming too close to each other.

THE SOLDIER

One would think that heaven took pleasure in poisoning the sad joys it granted you.

THE LEPER

But at least I was not alone. My sister's presence brought this retreat to life. I used to hear the sound of her footsteps in my loneliness. When I used to come out here at dawn to pray to God beneath these trees, the door of the tower would open softly, and my sister's voice would join imperceptibly with mine. In the evening, when I used to water my garden, she would sometimes stroll in the setting sun, here, in the very same spot where I am speaking to you now, and I would see her shadow pass back and forth over my flowers. Even when I didn't see her, I would find traces of her presence everywhere. Now I never come across any plucked flowers or small branches such as she might leave along my path in passing; I am alone; there is no longer any movement or life around me, and the path that led to her favorite grove is already disappearing under new grass. Without appearing to look after me, she incessantly took care to do things that might give me pleasure. I was often surprised, upon retiring to my room, to find a vase of new flowers or some beautiful fruit that she had nurtured herself. I dared not return the favors, however, and I had even begged her never to enter my room. But who can impose limits on a sister's affections? A single example will give you an idea of her fondness for me. One night, I was pacing back and forth in my cell, racked with terrible pain. In the middle of the night, having sat down momentarily to rest, I heard a faint noise at the entrance to my room. I approached, ears pricked, and to my great surprise I found my sister praying to God just outside my door. She had heard my moans; yet not wanting, in her delicacy, to disturb me, she came that she might be near me in case I should need her help. I heard her reciting the *Miserere* in a soft voice. I knelt down near the door, and without interrupting her, I followed her words in my mind. My eyes filled with tears: who would not have been moved by such affection? When I thought her prayer had ended, I said to her softly, "Good-by, dear sister, good-by. You can retire now; I feel a little better. May God bless you and reward you for your compassion!" She withdrew in silence. And surely her prayer was answered, for I finally enjoyed a few hours of peaceful sleep.

THE SOLDIER

How sad those first days after the death of your dear sister must have seemed to you!

THE LEPER

I remained a long time in a kind of daze that prevented me from feeling the full extent of my unhappiness; when at last I recovered, and was able to take stock of my situation, my reason nearly deserted me. That period will always be doubly sad for me, for it reminds me of my greatest misfortune and of the crime that almost became its consequence.

THE SOLDIER

Crime? I should not think you capable of committing one.

THE LEPER

It is all too true, and I am afraid that in telling you of this period of my life, I shall fall considerably in your esteem. Yet I do not wish to paint myself as better than I am; perhaps you will take pity on me as you condemn me. The thought of deliberately quitting this life had already occurred to me, during certain bouts of melancholy; yet the fear of God had always made me push it away. Then the simplest of circumstances, and one which would not have appeared likely to cause me distress, nearly damned

175

me for eternity. I had just suffered a new misfortune. For the past few years, a small dog had come into our lives: my sister had loved it dearly, and I must say that, after her passing, that poor animal became a real consolation for me. The creature's ugliness, no doubt, had determined its choice of our home as its refuge. He had been turned away by all; yet he was still a treasure in the leper's house. In recognition of the favor that God had granted us by sending us this friend, my sister named the dog *Miracle,* and this name, which contrasted with its ugly appearance, and the creature's perpetually good spirits, often helped us to forget our sorrows. Despite my attentions, the dog would run away occasionally, yet it never occurred to me that there might be any harm in this to anyone. Some townsfolk, however, became alarmed and feared the dog might give them the germ of my disease; they decided to lodge a complaint with the chief constable, who ordered that the dog be killed on the spot. A number of soldiers, accompanied by a few townspeople, came to my home at once to carry out this cruel order. They tied a rope around the animal's neck in my presence and dragged him away. When he was at the garden gate, I could not keep from looking at him one last time: I saw him turn his eyes to me to beg me for help, which I could not give him. They wanted to drown him in the river *Doria;* yet the townspeople, who were awaiting him outside, stoned him to death. I heard his cries, and returned to the tower more dead than alive. My trembling knees could no longer bear

176

my weight: I threw myself upon my bed in a state that I cannot describe. My sorrow would not let me see this just but harsh order as anything more than an abominable, useless act of barbarism; and though I am now ashamed of the feeling that motivated me then, I still cannot think of it without emotion. I spent the entire day in a state of tremendous agitation. The last living being had just been torn away from me, and this new blow had reopened all the wounds in my heart.

Such was my condition when, the same day, near sunset, I came to sit here, on the very stone on which you are now sitting. I had been reflecting awhile on my sorry fate when, over there, by those two birch trees that terminate the hedgerow, I saw two young newlyweds appear. They walked along the path, across the meadow, and passed close to me. That delightful tranquility which true happiness inspires was stamped on their beautiful faces; they walked slowly, their arms intertwined. Suddenly I saw them stop: the young woman leaned her head on her spouse's chest, and he took her rapturously into his arms. I felt my heart breaking. Shall I say it? For the first time in my life, envy crept into my heart. Never before had the image of happiness presented itself so powerfully to me. I followed them with my eyes to the end of the meadow, and was about to lose sight of them when some cries of delight reached my ears: it was their two families, who had come out to meet them. Grandparents, women, and children surrounded them: I heard a confused hum of joyful voices and saw the bright colors of their clothing amidst the trees. The entire group seemed enveloped in a cloud of happiness. I could not bear this sight; the torments of hell had entered my heart; I turned my eyes away, and rushed back to my cell. My God, how desolate, dark, and frightful it looked to me! Here, I said to myself, here is where my home shall always be! Here is where I shall drag out my deplorable life and await the belated end of my days! The Lord has spread happiness about, has spread it in torrents over all that breathes, and I, I alone! am without succor, without friends or companions. . . What a hideous fate!

Full of these gloomy thoughts, I forgot that there is a consoling being; I forgot myself. Why, I asked myself, was I ever allowed to see the light of day? Why is nature cruel and unjust only to me? Like a disinherited child, I have the rich patrimony of the human family before my eyes, but miserly heaven refuses me my share. No, no, I cried out at last in a fit of rage, there is no happiness for you on earth. Die, wretch, die! Too long have you sullied the earth with your presence; may she swallow you up alive and leave no trace of your odious existence! As my mad fury increased, the desire to destroy myself took hold of me and became the object of all my thoughts. At last, I resolved to set fire to my retreat, to let myself be consumed with all that might leave behind some memory of me. Restless and enraged, I ran out into the wild; I wandered a while in the shadows around my dwelling; involuntary howls escaped from my constricted breast, frightening even myself in the silence of the night. I returned to my abode still furious, crying out: Woe unto you, leper! Woe unto you! And, as though all things should contribute to my damnation, from the ruins of Bramafan Castle I heard the echo repeat distinctly: Woe unto you! I stopped, gripped with horror, at the door of the tower, and the faint echo of the mountain continued long afterward: Woe unto you!

I took a lamp and, determined to set fire to my home, I descended to the lowest room, bringing with me some vine shoots and dry twigs. It was the room my sister had lived in, and I had not entered it since her death: her armchair was still where I had left it when I had lifted her from it for the last time. I shuddered with dread upon seeing her veil and a few articles of her clothing scattered about the room. The last words she had uttered before leaving resurfaced in my memory: ''I will not abandon you when I die,'' she had said; ''Remember that I shall be present in your distress.'' Setting the lamp down on the table, I saw the string of the cross she used to wear round her neck, which she herself had placed between two pages of her Bible. At the sight of it, I recoiled in holy terror. The depth of the abyss into which I was about to cast myself became suddenly clear to my open eyes; trembling, I approached the sacred book. There it is! I cried. There is the succor she promised me! And as I was withdrawing the cross from the book, I found a sealed sheet with writing on it, which my good sister had left there for me. My tears, which had been held back by sorrow until that moment, burst forth in torrents: all my deadly plans vanished at once. I pressed that precious letter to my breast for a long time before I could read it; then, falling to my knees to beg for God's mercy, I opened it, and read, as I wept, the following words, which shall remain forever etched in my heart: *"My dear brother, I shall be leaving you soon, but I will never abandon you. From the heavens where I hope to go, I shall watch over you; I will pray God to give you the courage to endure life submissively until it pleases him to reunite us in another world. Then will I be able to show you all my affection; nothing more will prevent me from being near you, and nothing will keep us apart. I am leaving you my little cross, which I have worn all my life; it has often consoled me during my sufferings; my tears have had no other witness. Remember, when you see it, that my last wish was that you might live or die a good Christian!"* Precious letter! It shall never leave my presence: I will carry it with me to the grave: it will open up the gates of heaven, which my crime would have closed to me forever. As I finished reading it, I felt myself grow faint, exhausted by all I had just been through. I saw a cloud spread across my view, and for a short while I forgot all my afflictions, forgot I was even alive. When I came round, it was well into the night. As I began to think more clearly again, I felt an indescribable sense of peace. All that had happened that evening seemed like a dream to me. My first action was to raise my eyes to heaven in thanks for having saved me from the greatest of woes. Never had the firmament looked so serene and so beautiful: a star was shining outside my window; I contemplated it a long time with inexpressible pleasure, while thanking God for granting me the pleasure of still seeing it, and I felt secretly consoled by the thought that one of its beams was, after all, destined for the sad cell of the leper.

I went back to my room more at peace. I passed the rest of the night with the Book of Job, and the holy enthusiasm it brought to my soul finally dispelled, once and for all, the dark thoughts that had possessed me. I had never experienced such frightful moments when my sister was alive; knowing her to be near me was enough to make me calm again, and just the thought of her affection for me sufficed to console me and give me courage.

Compassionate stranger! May God save you from ever having to live alone! My sister and companion lives no more, yet heaven shall grant me the strength to endure life bravely. This shall it grant me, I hope, for I pray to it with all my heart.

THE SOLDIER

How old was your sister when you lost her?

THE LEPER

She was barely twenty-five, yet her suffering made her look older. And yet despite the illness that took her away, which had affected her appearance, she would still have been beautiful if not for her frightening pallor: she was an image of living death, and I could not look at her without sighing.

THE SOLDIER
She was very young to die.

THE LEPER
Her feeble, delicate constitution could not stand so many combined afflictions. I had noticed for some time that her death was imminent; indeed, so sad was her condition that I could not help but wish for it to come quickly. Seeing her languish and waste away with each passing day, I watched with a kind of grim joy as the end of her suffering drew near. She had been growing weaker and weaker for the past month; frequent fainting spells threatened her life every hour. One evening (it was around the beginning of August), she looked so frail that I didn't want to leave her side; she was seated in her armchair, having been unable for several days to stand her bed any longer. I sat down beside her, and in deepest darkness, we had our last conversation together. My tears would not stop; a cruel foreboding stirred my soul. "Why do you weep?" she said to me; "Why torment yourself so? I will not leave you when I die; I shall be present in your distress."

Moments later, she expressed the wish to be taken outside the tower, that she might say her prayers in her thicket of hazel trees, where she used to spend the greater part of the summer months. "I want," she said, "to die looking at the heavens." I did not, however, believe her hour to be so near. I took her in my arms to carry her away. "Just help me stand," she said; "I think I may yet have the strength to walk." I led her slowly as far as the hazel trees. Then I made a pillow for her with some dry leaves she had gathered herself and, having covered her with a veil to protect her from the night's dampness, I sat down beside her. But she wanted to be alone in her final meditation, and so I withdrew without letting her out of my sight. From time time to time I saw her veil rise and her white hands reach to the heavens. As I drew near to the thicket again, she asked me for water. I brought some in her cup; she wet her lips with it, but could not drink. "I feel the end approaching," she said to me, turning her head away. "Soon my thirst will be quenched forever. Give me strength, my brother, help your sister cross this desired but terrible threshold. Give me strength, recite the prayer for the dying." Those were her last words to me. I rested her head against my breast, and recited the prayer for the dying: "Pass on to eternity, dear sister!" I said to her; "Deliver yourself from this life, leave this skin that I hold in my arms!" For three hours I held her thus, assisting her in nature's final struggle; at last she expired, peacefully, and her soul departed from earth without effort.

The leper, at the end of his narrative, covered his face with his hands; the traveler was speechless with grief. After a moment of silence, the leper rose. *Stranger,* he said, *whenever sorrow or dejection should knock at your door, think of the hermit of the city of Aosta, and your visit to him will not have been in vain.*

They set off together toward the garden gate. As the soldier was about to leave, he put his glove on his right hand: "You have never shaken anyone's hand," he said to the leper. "Grant me the favor of shaking mine; it's the hand of a friend deeply interested in your fate." The leper recoiled several steps in a kind of horror and, raising his eyes and hands to the heavens, exclaimed: *Bountiful God! Shower your blessings on this compassionate man!*

"Grant me yet one more favor," continued the traveler. "I am about to depart; we shall not see each other again for a very long time perhaps. Could we not, with the necessary precautions of course, write to each other now and then? Such a correspondence might amuse you, and for my part it would bring me great pleasure. The leper reflected a moment. *Why,* he said, *should I seek to deceive myself? I ought to have no society but my own, no friend but God. We shall meet again in Him. Good-by, generous stranger, may you find happiness . . . Good-by forever!* The traveler left. The leper shut the gate and bolted it.

APPENDIXES

PREFACE (1811)

Joseph de Maistre

We have no wish to belittle the merits of those voyagers who came into the world before the one whose fascinating discoveries and adventures we are publishing here. *Magellen, Drake, Anson, Cook,* et alia were, no doubt, remarkable men; nevertheless, it is legitimate, and unless we are gravely mistaken, it is indeed our duty, to point out that the *Voyage Around My Room* possesses a particular merit that places it well above all preceding voyages. The most famous voyages can be repeated; they are traced on all the maps of the world by elegant dotted lines, and everyone is free to dash off along the trails blazed by these daring men. Such is not the case with the *Voyage Around My Room;* it has been done once and for all, and no mortal could ever dream of beginning it again, especially as the very country in which it took place no longer exists. That is to say, the most intrepid explorer, after exposing himself to unpleasant difficulties and errors of every sort, might at best find its four borders again; yet what is a country that has only borders? For its interior, which has irretrievably vanished; for the number and organization of its provinces; for its internal administration; for its natural products; and for anything of interest that occurred in that unknown region, one can only refer back to the voyager who described it, or else resign oneself to knowing nothing more about it. Skepticism on this matter would leave a fatal lacuna, a veritable *chasm* in the geography and history of the human spirit.

Fortunately, this voyage so patently bears the seal of truth that we have little to fear from the Pyrrhonism of the most difficult readers. Unless we have been utterly seduced by the interest aroused in us by the *circumvoyager* (and why not call him thus? We have certainly been recommended to say *circumnavigator*), it seems to us that his good faith and frankness shine through each line in such a manner as to inspire conviction, and we have no doubt that he should win the most complete and best deserved confidence of any honest reader.

As for those ill-organized minds who have dared to include the *Voyage Around My Room* among the ranks of imaginary voyages, we sincerely pity them: one would have to be of rather blunted sensibility, and quite unfamiliar with the sentiment of truth, to judge thus a work in which every page *sparkles with realities*. From Mme de Hautcastel to Rosine, there is not a single actor in this voyage who is not real. We here assume the solemn task of rigorously demonstrating this, since Europe itself seems to desire it.

Metaphysics is a science rarely encountered along the routes of explorers. And yet, by an exception that does great honor to the author of the *Voyage Around*

My Room, one finds therein a whole system of transcendental philosophy; and even the ladies, who do not like and rarely read large books, will learn from it as much about the *critique of the soul* as the late professor Kant, of nebulous memory, once knew.

We will not lavish too much praise on the style of the work, which is quite something all the same. Rather, we would hope not to be deemed immoderate if we say merely that our voyager writes as well as Captain Cook.

By a singular twist of fate, the author was never able to oversee any of the numerous editions of his voyage, and even at the present time, he is forced to place his trust in us for this new edition, rendered absolutely necessary by the great number of errors that marred the prior editions and which could have had grave consequences.

We keenly wish we could let the public know who the author of this voyage is, but he has judged it appropriate to conceal his name. Although we have received some rather pressing conjectures in this regard, we will not venture to publish them, having always considered such liberties to be veritable improprieties. We shall attempt merely to allay the justified concerns of an estimable man who long trembled in fear of being falsely taken for the author of the *Voyage Around My Room.*

In December of 1810, there arose, between two French men of letters of a most venerable age, a very lively dispute as to the question of *which of the two had been booed the first on the stages of Paris.* The

two adversaries fought over this honor in the newspapers with extraordinary ferocity.

> Never had we seen, nor read, nor heard tell
> Of points of honor taking such a form.

Yet we will not enter into an examination of this
question, which does not concern us; we merely
thought it necessary to grant close attention to a
note in which M. Ximenez declares in explicit terms
"that he has assumed the title of *dean of French
dramatic authors*" (which was what gave rise to
the quarrel between him and M. *Portelance*), "to
distinguish himself from another Ximenez who
has written several works published in Paris in 1794
and thereafter, including a *Voyage Around My
Room.*"[1]

It would, no doubt, be irksome for M. Ximenez to
pass innocently for an author he considered to be
passably insipid, as we may recall having read in a
number of newspapers of the time. First of all, however, we doubt that this century, no matter how
dreadfully corrupt it may be, could have produced
even one man so unjust as to attribute the *Voyage
Around My Room* to M. *Augustin Ximenez.*

We should, moreover, understand the venerable
author's fears had this voyage been published under
the name of *Ximenez.* Yet on the frontispieces of the

---

[1].In the *Journal de Paris* of 7 December 1810, no. 341, page
2419 (note), M. Ximenez claims to be eighty-five years old, while
his rival, he says, is only seventy-seven.

previous editions, one reads only the letter X, followed by an ellipsis. Now, while allowing that one may legitimately take this letter to be the initial of the author's name, we should greatly inconvenience the worthy *dean of French dramatic authors* if we were to call upon him, with due ceremony, to explain to us by what manner of reasoning he has managed to convince himself that every man whose name begins with an X must perforce be called *Ximenez*.

Lastly, even if we explained this mysterious letter which has been so troubling him for twenty years, we still would not have said the author's name. It was quite enough in the beautiful lands where this memorable voyage was undertaken and concluded with such courage, patience, and happiness. It was enough above all in the gentle circle of friends for whom this voyage was written: it has no individual meaning anywhere else.

Often in society we have heard the question asked: *How can it be that the author of the* Voyage Around My Room *has never published another work?* The answer is brief, but decisive: *He had other things to do. Graphomania* is a strange disease of our century. An author writes one hundred volumes, of which at least sixty will be forgotten or even burned by posterity. No doubt it would have been better if he had not written them. The great authors of the great century,[2] duly stereotyped, can fit in the pockets of a

---

[2].The age of Louis XIV. (Translator's note)

waistcoat, while one of our contemporary authors will sometimes require an armoire all to himself if he is to fit comfortably: it is a terrible custom. Are we put on this world only to write? One must also live, sleep, visit one's friends, and one must even make war: it's a worthy trade, though it appreciably hinders literary activities.

Meanwhile, we have by chance obtained a small work issued from the idle pen of the same author. It is called *The Leper of the City of Aosta,* and one may read it at the back of this new edition of the *Voyage Around My Room.*

While these two plants do not belong to the same class, we thought it proper to bring them together, for they were born of the same soil, and we hope that by leaning against each other they will more easily stand up straight.

We could add an infinity of other things still, all of the highest importance, for the advancement of human knowlege. We shall omit them, however, in accordance with the opinion (to which we defer) that a preface must always be a little shorter than the book.

NOTES AND VARIANTS

Note on the Texts

For the translation of *Voyage autour de ma chambre,* I have used principally the original edition from the Bibliothèque Nationale et Universitaire de Strasbourg as reproduced in Xavier de Maistre, *Nouvelles,* edited by Pierre Dumas, Piero Cazzola, and Jacques Lovie (Editions Slatkine, Geneva 1984); for the sake of comparison (the differences being negligible), I occasionally referred to the text of the 1825 edition of the author's *Oeuvres complètes,* reproduced in Xavier de Maistre, *Voyage autour de ma chambre,* (Collection des Cent chefs d'oeuvre, Robert Laffont, Paris 1959), as well as the recent reproduction of the 1811 edition (Collection Romantique No. 9, Jose Cortí, Paris, 1991). In those cases where my translation (based on the Strasbourg text) differs from the 1811 and 1825 texts, I have indicated this in the notes below.

The translation of *Expedition nocturne autour de ma chambre,* on the other hand, combines both the 1825 edition as it appears in the *Voyage autour de ma chambre* collection (Paris, 1959), as well as the text that appears in *Nouvelles* (Geneva, 1984), which is from an autograph manuscript kept at the Moscow Archives containing a number of interesting variants eventually deleted for the original edition that appeared in the *Oeuvres complètes* in 1825. In general, it was clear to me why those passages were struck from the text in that edition, as most of them were superfluous and added little or nothing aesthetically to the work. For the most part I have respected those choices in my translation, while presenting the more interesting deleted passages in the notes that follow. In one particular instance, however—the Ossian chapter—I have reproduced the text as it appears in the Moscow manuscript, because the author himself said in a letter that he had regretted that deletion and that "this jest on the baroque names of Ossian's heroes is no worse than the rest," and because I myself found the passage too amusing to relegate to an end note.

The translation of the *Lepreux de la Cité d'Aoste* was instead based entirely on the version in the 1825 edition, as it appears in the Jose Cortí reprint (Paris, 1991).

The reader may also note some oddities in the punctuation and typefaces of the *Voyage Around My Room,* such as the excessive use of long dashes and italics, which then disappear for the most part in the *Nocturnal Expedition Around My Room.* This typographical inconsistency is a fair reflection of the original; my decision to reproduce it in translation was predicated on the simple fact that De Maistre, in the *Voyage,* was clearly trying to imitate the style of Laurence Sterne in *Tristram Shandy.* To suppress such a distinguishing feature merely to conform to contemporary tastes would have necessarily impoverished the text by depriving it of a reference fundamental to its conception.

S.S.

Voyage Around My Room

Page 3. Epigraph: "In many an author of great learning I have read / that one gains nothing by roaming the world too much." Jean Baptiste Louis Gresset (1709–77) was a French poet and author of mordant wit, and a member of the French Academy.

in petto: It., literally, "in my chest." De Maistre's occasional Italianisms and preoccupations with Italian culture stems from his living in Turin, then capital of the Kingdom of Sardinia and ruled by the House of Savoy.

Page 8. Giovambattista Beccaria (1716–81), a member of the Order of Piarists and a physicist whose important studies in electricity, in the wake of Benjamin Franklin, eventually earned him membership in the Royal Society of London. He was commissioned in 1759 to measure the length of one degree of a longitudinal arc in the Piedmont.

Page 12. In French, *bête* (beast) and *âme* (soul) are both feminine nouns, and on several occasions in this text De Maistre effectively uses their gender to personify both concepts. I have ascribed masculinity to the beast to avoid the awkwardness that would result from referring to the actions of the narrator's beast in the world—the actions of a man—in the feminine; for the soul, on the other hand, I have opted to preserve the feminine gender of the original, as it presented no such practical difficulties.

Page 27. The teachings of Martinez Pasqualis (1715?–1779), or Martines de Pasqually, a shadowy figure of uncertain origin, though probably of Portuguese-Jewish extraction. A magus and theurge, gnostic and mystagogue, Martinez had a great influence on 18th-century French Illuminism. The practice of Martinism involved, among other things, the evocation of spirits, elemental and otherwise. Martinez expounded his teachings with the aid of such famous pupils as Louis Claude de Saint-Martin and the Marquise de la Croix. His central work was a *Treatise on the Reintegration of Beings*.

Page 28. According to tradition, the tomb of Empedocles is Mount Aetna, into whose mouth the pre-Socratic philosopher is said to have cast himself to prove to his contemporaries that he had ascended to heaven, since he expected that no remains of his body would be found. The volcano, however, supposedly had the last word, coughing his sandals back up intact.

Page 33. Charlotte and Albert are characters in Goethe's *The Sorrows of Young Werther*.

Page 36. See *The Sorrows of Young Werther*, letter 28, August 12. (Note from the 1817 edition of *Voyage autour de ma chambre*.)

Jenny is Jeanne Baptiste de Maistre (1762–1824), Xavier's sister.

Count Ugolino della Gherardesca was a 13th-century lord of Pisa, a Ghibelline by family tradition but for a period a Guelph for politial expediency. As a result of political intrigues and struggles, Ugolino was imprisoned together with two sons and two grandsons in the Gualandi tower (''the tower of hunger'') by his rival, Archbishop Ruggiero Ubaldini, and left there to starve to death. Having been the last to die, Ugolino is said to have attempted to survive by eating the flesh of his sons. This episode inspired one of the more horrific scenes of Dante's *Inferno*.

Page 37. Louis, chevalier d'Assas, captain of the Auvergne regiment. A French national hero, on the eve of the battle of Klostercamp (Prussia), during the night of October 15, 1760, he went alone into a wood near the French encampment to search for signs of a surprise attack. Finding himself suddenly surrounded by enemy soldiers, who held their bayonets to his chest and threatened him with death if he should make a sound, the brave Assas sacrificed himself for the safety of the army when he gave the now famous cry: *"A moi, Auvergne, ce sont les ennemis!"* ("Help, Auvergne, it's the enemy!").

Page 39. . . . *my uncle Toby's Hobby-Horse:* a reference to Laurence Sterne's *Tristram Shandy*. Clearly, painting is De Maistre's own "hobby-horse."

Page 42. This is probably a reference to the portrait known as *La Fornarina* ("The Baker's Daughter"), now in the Uffizi. The young woman portrayed has been traditionally presumed to be the painter's mistress.

Page 43. The preceding two paragraphs were not in the 1825 edition.

Page 46. Apelles, born at Colophon in Ionia in the first half of the fourth century B.C., was reputed to be the greatest painter of antiquity.

Page 52. Madame Repous was a famous fashion designer at the time of *Voyage autour de ma chambre*. (Note from the 1817 edition)

Athaliah, queen of Judah (2 Kings XI, 1–16), daughter of Ahab and Jezebel, was wife of King Joram, son of Jehosaphat. Upon the death of Ahaziah, her son and king after Joram's death, she ascended to the throne after having all of Ahaziah's sons murdered, save Joash, whom the priest Jehoiada took in and eventually restored to the throne by inciting the people to slaughter Athaliah. De Maistre's mention of her dream is a reference to Racine's drama *Athalie*.

197

Page 53. This chapter was written in 1794.

Page 55. The author did not keep his word, and if something with this title was in fact published, the author of *Voyage autour de ma chambre* claims he had nothing to do with it. (Note from the 1817 edition)

Page 60. A reference to the heroine of Richardson's *Clarissa* and to the Charlotte of Goethe's *Werther*.

Mr. Cleveland: a reference to the protagonist of *L'Histoire de Monsieur Cleveland ou le Philosophe anglais (1732–1739)*, translated by the abbé Prévost, the story of which takes place in the United States, among various Indian tribes.

Page 61. The *assemblée des Notables* was a gathering of the most important figures in the kingdom, chosen from the clergy, the nobility, and the bourgeoisie, to whom the king would turn for advice in times of crisis when failing to convene the Estates General. De Maistre may be referring to the 1787 convocation of the *assemblée* by Calonne, the Comptroller General, who failed miserably in his intentions and had to flee to England.

Page 65. Xavier de Maistre's father, François Xavier de Maistre, a prominent judge and deeply religious man, was the beloved father of ten children. The bust mentioned here has been preserved in the De Maistre family.

Page 66. *the island at our antipodes:* probably a reference to Sardinia, which at the time, being the southernmost province of the kingdom of the same name, would have been the "antipodes" of the capital city of Turin, at the northern end of the realm.

Page 73. The preceding paragraph was not in the 1825 edition.

Page 74. Ranson was a well known physician in Turin

at the time this chapter was written. (Note from the 1817 edition)

Page 75. Eusebio Valli (1755–1816) was an Italian physician and epidemiologist. His experiments with frogs in searching for a cure for rabies were instrumental in its later discovery, though his own efforts bore no immediate fruit.

Luigi Antonio Caraccioli (1721–1803) was an Oratorian and the distinguished author of the so-called *Letters of Pope Clement XIV*.

Jean François Cigna (1734–91) was professor at the University of Turin and the founder of a literary and scientific society that was to become the Academy of Sciences of Turin.

Page 76. *his lovely companion:* i. e., Aspasia, Pericles' mistress.

Page 77. William Harvey (1578–1657) was an English physician famous for discovering the circulation of the blood; Lazzaro Spallanzani (1729–99) was an Italian naturalist known for his important work on the circulatory and digestive systems, and on microorganisms.

"Protophysician" was a commonly used title in the legislation of the kingdom of Sardinia, which makes this a purely topical joke on the author's part. (Note from the 1817 edition)

Nocturnal Expedition Around My Room

Page 85. Georges Louis Leclerc, comte de Buffon (1707–88), was a celebrated naturalist and author of his day, and wrote an important *Histoire Naturelle*. From his acceptance speech to the French Academy in 1753 (also called

Discourse on Style) comes the famous expression, *"Le style est l'homme même"* (which is very often mistakenly quoted as *"Le style, c'est l'homme"*).

Page 86. In the Moscow manuscript, this is the rue Saint-Thérèse.

Page 87. The Piedmont fell in 1796. Napoleon's Italian campaign was fought in 1797, and the king of Sardinia withdrew to that island in 1798, leaving his officers behind without any specific duties.

Page 90. That room was situated in the citadel of Turin; the new "voyage" was undertaken some time after it had fallen to Austro-Russian forces. (Note from various early editions)

The star that "disappeared" would presumably be the seventh in the constellation, generally less visible to the naked eye; modern telescopy shows that there are far more stars present.

Page 93. Marie, like Mme de Hautcastel, remains unidentified, though she may be the same Marie Barrillier mentioned on page 128 as "Elisa."

Page 94. A *Second Voyage autour de ma chambre* was published by an anonymous author.

Page 97. The Superga is a hill just outside of Turin at the summit of which stands a magnificent basilica built between 1717 and 1731 from plans by Filippo Juvara; the construction of the church commemorated the lifting of the siege of Turin by the French in 1706. It is also the burial place of the princes of the house of Savoy, kings of Sardinia.

Page 99. One of the most illustrious Athenian orators, Demosthenes (384–322 B.C.) used to practice by reciting long passages with his mouth full of pebbles.

Page 100. The above passage, from "I soon noticed" (p. 99) to "masterpiece" is from the Moscow manuscript. In traditional editions of the *Expedition* it is shortened as follows:

"I noticed that this method indeed excited my imagination, and gave me an inner sense of poetic ability that I should certainly have exploited successfully to compose my dedicatory epistle in verse, etc . . ."

Page 102. It.: "He's mad, by Bacchus, he's mad!" In the Moscow manuscript, this paragraph is followed by another:

"With these words he fled, murmuring to himself in dismay; he fled down the corridor like a dark whirlwind, the sound of his steps resembling that of a rock which, split from Demardo by the lightning, bounds down the mountain's steep slope, the sound of his confused voice resembling that of the straining wind as it groans in the gorges of Lunc."

A friend of Plato, Archytas was a Pythagorean philosopher and mathematician with a keen interest in music and mechanics. He is said to have invented, among other things, the screw, the pulley, and the rattle.

Page 105. Franz Josef Gall (1758–1828), German physician and inventor of the dubious science of phrenology.

Page 106. . . . *too much:* In the Moscow manuscript, this paragraph was followed by three more, passages of which were revised and included in the final edition. The three paragraphs were originally as follows:

"I confess in all innocence that I was rather proud of having made [this discovery]; moreover, to verify it and turn it immediately to account, I would give myself another contusion even greater than the first, and thereby

201

honorably acquit myself of the task of composing my dedi-catory epistle. To this end, I removed the portrait of Mme de Hautcastel, which was directly in front of me, lest I should put a hole in it, and, taking aim at a rather level spot on the wall between two prints, I drew back to the far end of the room to get a running start, determined either to split my head apart or to begin my poetic career with a sublime bit of verse.

"Walking backward in this fashion, I encountered my bed and fell down on it in a sitting position; as my hand had perchance come down upon my nightcap, I decided to cover my head with it and go to bed.

CHAPTER XII

"My friends, ever mindful of my glory, will doubtless regret that I failed to carry my adventure to its conclusion, while the envious will perhaps accuse me of fickleness, for having so suddenly changed my mind. I would have them know, however, that while I was stepping back to get a running start, several rather sensible thoughts occurred to me, and prevented me from proceeding. I realized that in cracking my head, I was not absolutely certain to crack it poetically; secondly, I was even less certain that it might not already be somehow cracked, which made the experi-ment rather dangerous. Moreover, the fear of frightening my fair neighbor a second time by the noise I should have made in knocking my head against the wall would have sufficed to thwart my designs despite all the advantages I might gain from it. In short, it occurred to me—though it occurs all too seldom to most people—that the art of mak-ing verse is not an absolute necessity for anyone and that it was enough for me, and for my reputation, to have discovered the art of being a poet at will by means of a new method which I can employ whenever I please—wherefore one may reasonably surmise that if I continue to write in prose, it can only be out of modesty.''

Page 109. Jocrisse is a character from traditional French farces, the typical fool who is often the butt of others' jokes. Scapin is a character from the Italian *Commedia dell'Arte* (known as Scapino in It.), introduced into French comedy by Molière in *Les Fourberies de Scapin;* Scapino is the typically shrewd, scheming valet.

Page 114. Probably Sophie Zagriatska, Xavier de Maistre's wife.

Page 124. As the story goes, Virginia was the daughter of Virginius, a centurion. Around 450 B.C., when the decemvirs had been appointed to publish a code of laws, Appius Claudius, one of the decemvirs, intended to seduce Virginia; to get her into his possession, he had one of his dependents claim her as a slave belonging to his own household. Appius Claudius presided over the case himself, and judged in favor of his dependent. As Virginia was being taken away, her father stabbed her to death, preferring her death to her dishonor, and said: ''Appius, by this innocent blood I consign your head to the gods of Tartarus.'' The act was followed by a popular uprising in which the decemvirs were overthrown and more democratic laws instituted. The death of Virginia was a subject treated by many, including Livy, Petrarch, Chaucer, Alfieri, and Lethière.

Page 127. In the Moscow manuscript, this chapter began with two additional paragraphs:

"My general fondness for the entire female sex notwithstanding, I must own that I retain a certain preference for my good vestal: she is one of my favorite conquests, and I know not what natural penchant leads me to pay her court. One might conclude, on the basis of this admission, that there is a certain monotony in my love affairs, since I keep coming back to the same adventures. Far from it! I would have you know, in fact, that unforeseen incidents, though with the same characters, are forever befalling me, occurrences that continually vary the scene, making it each time as interesting as it is novel.—As an example of this, I will tell you of the catastrophe to which I nearly fell victim with this same vestal.

"One night—it makes me shudder even now—still awake after waiting several hours in vain for sleep to come, I amused myself chatting with the unlucky girl, to allow her time to recover her strength. Stirred by a prophetic spirit, I was telling her that more than twenty centuries after the Roman senate sentenced her to death, and under the rule of consuls of another sort, the customs would be vastly improved and very few women would be buried alive for the crime of which she had been so ignobly accused—when all of a sudden, her eyes closed and her waxen face fell forward onto her breast. She was fainting! Nearby there happened to be, according to the custom, a vase of water; I thought I was helping her by suggesting that she drink a little of it: how imprudent! Alas! Her friends, hoping in their compassion to shorten her agony, had poisoned the water. The luckless vestal went into frightful convulsions and breathed her last in my arms. Imagine my distress! In my despair, I swallowed the rest of the fatal beverage, and its soporific poison made me sleep so deeply that I did not reawaken until noon the next day.''

Page 128. Elisa was the pen name of Marie Barrillier, a poetess from Aosta.

Page 136. *Sur le bonheur des sots* (''On the happiness of idiots''), Paris, 1872.

Page 139. Palus Maeotis was the ancient name for the Sea of Azov.

Page 140. The author was serving in Piedmont when the Savoy, his birthplace, was reunited with France. (Note from various editions)

Page 143. An obvious reference to Chateaubriand. As the latter's *Voyage en Amerique* was not published until 1827, De Maistre at this time could only have known of his descriptions of America from *Atala* (1801) or possibly *Les Natchez* (1815).

Page 144. Themistocles, a great Athenian statesman and military leader, commanded the Greek fleet in their victory over the Persians at Salamis in 480 B.C.

Page 147. A line is an obsolete unit of measurement equal to one-twelfth of an inch.

Page 151. A popular air that lent itself to improvisation, and on which numerous composers, including Marin Marais, wrote variations.

Page 154. The Moscow manuscript contained one more paragraph:

''At last I stepped down from my horse, bringing half of my saddle with me to use as a pillow, and I got into bed, my heart and mind perfectly at peace, filled with the sweet sensation of that just and noble pride which one inevitably experiences upon concluding a difficult and perilous undertaking somewhat successfully and quite irreproachably. Indeed, if the reader would recall to mind all the reflections I have shared with him, as well as the discreet and modest behavior I observed in all my various encounters—with one of the most beautiful women in Turin, with her slipper, and with several different constellations—he could not help but admit that neither the most rigorous moralist nor the most priggish of prudes would ever take exception to anything therein.''

CHRONOLOGY

1763. Xavier de Maistre is born on November 8 to François Xavier Joseph Marie Maistre, son of lord Maistre, public prosecutor and second president of the Sovereign Senate of the Savoy (in 1780 he would be granted the title of count).

1773. He spends a happy childhood at La Bauche, a village in the Echelles canton. Xavier receives his education from the parish priest, showing great intellectual curiosity but little desire to apply himself.

That same year Victor Amadeus III succeeds Charles Emmanuel III as king of Sardinia.

1774. King Louis XV of France dies, succeeded by Louis XVI.

1781. At age 18, Xavier de Maistre decides upon a military career.

1783. The first hot-air balloon, called a Montgolfière after its inventors, the brothers Montgolfier, is successfully flown.

1784. On May 5 Xavier flies in a hot-air balloon with a friend. He describes this amusingly in a *Letter containing an account of the aerostatic experiment of Chambéry.*

1784–86. He is garrisoned in the Piedmont, at Exilles and at Pignerol (where he has vague intentions of writing a novel on the man in the iron mask, who was imprisoned in the fortress there). He leads a contented and carefree existence, reading the French philosophers and Goethe's *Werther,* and writing light verse; with a friend he dreams of constructing wings out of batiste and flying to America.

1787. He is stationed in Turin, to his great delight.

1789. Beginning of the French Revolution. The comte d'Artois arrives in Turin with a group of émigrés from France.

1790. On the eve of Carnival, Xavier crosses swords with a Piedmontese officer, Petono de Meïran. He emerges victorious, but is put under house arrest for forty-two days. To amuse himself, he writes *Voyage autour de ma chambre*.

1791. Antiroyalist pamphlets, coming out of a Savoyard Jacobin, begin to circulate in the Piedmont.

In March, Xavier leaves Turin for Fenestrella.

1792. In September, French troops invade the Savoy. The Sardinian army falls back behind the Alps. In October, the National Assembly of Allobroges orders all military personnel fighting under the banner of the ''tyrant of Sardinia'' to return home under threat of being declared émigrés.

Xavier refuses to renounce the royalist cause.

1793. In August, Sardinian troops under the command of the Austrian de Vins penetrate the Savoy but are driven back by Maréchal Kellermann. Xavier fights courageously.

1794. Xavier goes to visit his brother Joseph at Lausanne, Switzerland. He leaves him the manuscript of the *Voyage*.

1795. In April, Joseph publishes the *Voyage autour de ma chambre* in Lausanne. Xavier, promoted to the rank of captain, is in the Alps with the troops defending the Val d'Aoste.

1796. Napoleon forces the king of Sardinia to agree to the armistice of Cherasco. In accordance with the Treaty of Paris (May 15), the king cedes the duchy of Savoy, and the counties of Nice, Tende, and Beuil. In October, Charles Emmanuel IV succeeds Victor Amadeus III.

1798. In December, Charles Emmanuel abdicates.

Xavier leaves Aoste. He returns to Turin, rue de la Providence, and begins the first draft of the *Expédition nocturne autour de ma chambre*.

1799. The Russian marshal Suvorov arrives at Verona in April and forces the French to leave Turin in June. Austria, however, opposes the restoration of Charles Emmanuel IV to the Sardinian throne. The Piedmont falls to Austria.

Xavier, who had served as a staff officer of Suvorov, decides to emigrate.

1800. Czar Paul I orders Suvorov to return to Russia, promising a triumphal welcome. Then in a fit of whimsy, he heaps disgrace on him. Xavier loyally follows the old marshal to his St. Petersburg retreat, where the old man dies in his arms in May.

1801. On the night of March 23, Paul I is assassinated. His son Alexander succeeds him.

Xavier sets up a studio in Moscow as a painter-portraitist.

1803. His brother Joseph arrives at St. Petersburg as plenipotentiary delegate of the king of Sardinia.

1805. Thanks to Joseph, Xavier is appointed director of the Admiralty (museum, library, physics laboratory).

1807. Napoleon defeats the Russians at Friedland.

1809. Xavier, who remained a soldier even while serving as director, is made a colonel in August. At his brother's insistence, he resumes religious practices.

1810. Xavier completes and publishes *Le Lèpreux de la*

Cité d'Aoste. He fights in Georgia against insurgents and Turks.

1811. Serves in the Caucasus. The *Le Lèpreux* and the *Voyage* are published together in St. Petersburg.

1812. Returning north, Xavier battles Napoleon's troops, and describes in his letters the horror of the Great Army's retreat.

1813. He marries Sophia Zagriatska.

1814. Napoleon ("the man from Hell") abdicates.

1815. The Hundred Days. Waterloo.

1815–16. Xavier is sent to Finland. Bored, he gives up the military career.

1817. He lives a tranquil family life at St. Petersburg. He has a son.

Voyage autour de ma chambre is republished in Paris.

1821. His brother Joseph dies in Turin.

1825 The *Oeuvres complètes de Xavier de Maistre* is published in Paris, and meets with considerable success.

1826. Returns to the Savoy and revisits his beloved Turin, where he is given a hero's welcome. For a dozen years he leads the life of an important man of the world.

1837. His only son, Arthur, dies.

1838. He leaves Italy. Passes through Nice, Chambéry, and Saint-Point (where he visits the poet Lamartine, a relation of his). In Paris, in November, he meets Sainte-Beuve.

1839. Returns to Russia. His St. Petersburg salon is the meeting place of a glamorous French set.

1851. His wife dies, leaving him despondent.

1852. Xavier de Maistre dies peacefully in his sleep, at St. Petersburg, on the night of June 12–13.